Was Superman a SPY?

Meredith Berrett

BRIAN CRONIN is the writer and producer of the Comics Should Be Good blog at Comic Book Resources (www .cbr.cc). He has been writing the online column "Comic Book Urban Legends Revealed" since June 2005. He has a JD from Fordham Law School and is a practicing attorney in the state of New York. He lives in New York, where he enjoys writing about himself in the third person. For more legends about the world of sports and pop culture, check out www.legendsrevealed.com.

Was Superman a SPY?

AND OTHER COMIC BOOK LEGENDS REVEALED

BRIAN CRONIN

A PLUME BOOK

PLUME
Published by the Penguin Group
Penguin Group (USA) Inc., 375 Hudson Street, New York, New York 10014, U.S.A. •
Penguin Group (Canada), 90 Eglinton Avenue East, Suite 700, Toronto, Ontario, Canada
M4P 2Y3 (a division of Pearson Penguin Canada Inc.) • Penguin Books Ltd., 80 Strand,
London WC2R 0RL, England • Penguin Ireland, 25 St. Stephen's Green, Dublin 2,
Ireland (a division of Penguin Books Ltd.) • Penguin Group (Australia), 250 Camberwell
Road, Camberwell, Victoria 3124, Australia (a division of Pearson Australia Group Pty.
Ltd.) • Penguin Books India Pvt. Ltd., 11 Community Centre, Panchsheel Park, New
Delhi – 110 017, India • Penguin Group (NZ), 67 Apollo Drive, Rosedale, North Shore
0632, New Zealand (a division of Pearson New Zealand Ltd.) • Penguin Books (South
Africa) (Pty.) Ltd., 24 Sturdee Avenue, Rosebank, Johannesburg 2196, South Africa

Penguin Books Ltd., Registered Offices: 80 Strand, London WC2R 0RL, England

First published by Plume, a member of Penguin Group (USA) Inc.

First Printing, May 2009
1 3 5 7 9 10 8 6 4 2

Copyright © Brian Cronin, 2009
All rights reserved

Pages 241–244 constitute an extension of this copyright page.

℗ REGISTERED TRADEMARK—MARCA REGISTRADA

LIBRARY OF CONGRESS CATALOGING-IN-PUBLICATION DATA

Cronin, Brian.
    Was Superman a spy? / Brian Cronin.
        p. cm.
    Includes bibliographical references.
    ISBN 978-0-452-29532-2
    1. Comic books, Strips, etc.—Unites States.   2. Comic strip characters—United
States.   3. Common fallacies—United States.   I. Title.
    PN6725.C76   2009
    741.5'973--dc22   2008030601

Printed in the United States of America
Set in Iowan Oldstyle
Designed by Chris Welch

For my grandfather, Bernard Flynn

"Knowledge is the food of the soul."
—PLATO

Contents

Contents

Part III
OTHER COMIC BOOK COMPANIES

Acknowledgments

Love and thanks to Meredith, my parents, and my siblings for their love and support.

Thanks to my agent, Rick Broadhead; my editor, John Mihaly; my editor at Plume, Branda C. Maholtz; Rob Williams; Joanne Lue; Celly Ryan; the Grand Comic Book Database for supplying cover images (www.comics.org); Jonah Weiland and Comic Book Resources; and the rest of my gang at Comics Should Be Good! (the Gregs, Brad, Bill, Mark, Pol, and Danielle).

Thanks specifically to the following people who helped suggest or provide information for the stories in this book: John McDonagh (easily the number one reader for suggesting legends), Mark Evanier, Roy Thomas, Michael Eury, J. M. DeMatteis (the most generous creator I know), Paul Newell, Todd VerBeek, Jason, Marc, Linda Burns, Greg Theakston, Reilly Brown, Jim MacQuarrie, Daniel Best, TV's Grady, Hoosier X, Michael Bailey, Tom DeFalco, RAB, Michael Grabois, Todd Gilchrist, Randall Bytwerk, Jeremy Goldstone, Glen Cadigan, Robert Pincombe, LtMarvel, Mark Arnold, Tony Isabella, Roger Stern, Jim Shooter, Michael E, Mark Seddon, Daniël van Eijmeren, Joe Simon, Randy Schueller, David Gerstein, Scott Rowland, Jakob, Matthew Johnson, Jim, and Edward Summer.

Acknowledgments

Finally, thanks to all my English teachers and professors for getting me this far: Eleanor Spillett, Kevin Kavanah, Lizabeth Cooke, Ann Slocum, Randall Craig, Teresa Ebert, Jonathan Schiff, Donald Faulkner, Mike Hill, Carolyn Yalkut, and Judith Fetterley.

Introduction

Amusingly enough, it all began with falling for an urban legend myself. A few years ago, I wrote on my comic blog, Comics Should Be Good! about comic writer-artist Walter Simonson's run on the comic book title *Fantastic Four* in the late 1980s and early 1990s. I made a comment regarding Simonson's distaste for the ways some writers had handled the Fantastic Four's most famous villain, Doctor Doom, over the years. Simonson had written a story that could explain away many of these appearances as having been made by impostors. I had read more than once that Simonson privately kept a list of the character's appearances that he specifically felt should be ignored. Well, sometime after my comments were published, I received an e-mail from—who else?—Walter Simonson!

Simonson kindly pointed out that he had never made any such list but that he repeatedly had heard people refer to the supposed list! Simonson specifically noted how bemused he was at the fact that he himself was the subject of an "urban legend." While chagrined over my error, it occurred to me that there were plenty of comic-book-related stories out there that have been passed around for years without being checked out, so I decided it would be a great idea to either confirm or debunk them. In June 2005 I began a weekly column on the topic.

Three years and over 500 urban legends later, here we are with a collection of 130 comic book stories—65 of my favorite legends from the column plus 65 brand-new legends! Some of them are false and some of them are true, but all of them demonstrate the fascinating history of comic books.

In an effort to make it easier to find the legend you're looking for, I've split them into three parts: one for legends related to DC Comics, one for those related to Marvel Comics, and one for legends related to all the other great comic book companies out there.

I had a lot of fun compiling these stories, and I hope you have a lot of fun reading them!

Part One
DC Comics

DC Comics began in 1937 as a deal between pulp magazine publisher Harry Donenfeld and comic book publisher Major Malcolm Wheeler-Nicholson, who needed Donenfeld's financing to publish his latest project, *Detective Comics* #1 (hence the DC part of DC Comics). Donenfeld owned DC Comics and had a partnership with Wheeler-Nicholson's original comic book company, National Allied Publications, as well as with Max Gaines's All-American Publications. (Another early comic innovator, Gaines may have been the very first person to actually think of charging for comic books—the earliest comic books were designed as promotional giveaways.)

All three companies published together under a loose partnership, calling themselves National Comics. Donenfeld soon bought out Wheeler-Nicholson, and in 1944 he bought out All-American Publications as well. By this time, while officially going by the name National Publications, the company was known colloquially as DC Comics, and DC is what appeared on the logos of the books. The company would not take the name officially, though, until the late 1970s.

Donenfeld and his former accountant Jack Liebowitz ran the company (though Donenfeld's son, Irwin Donenfeld, eventually took over for his father) until, in 1967, it was purchased by Kinney National Services, which quickly changed its name to Warner Bros. after it acquired the famed Warner Bros. movie studio as well. DC Comics is currently a subsidiary of Warner Bros. Entertainment, which has turned a number of its comic book properties into films and television series.

1

SUPERMAN

Jerry Siegel and Joe Shuster, two teenagers from Cleveland, had pitched their idea for a comic strip called *Superman* to a number of different comic strip distributors, but to no avail. Their story about an alien who came to Earth from a dying world and (while secretly pretending to be a meek newspaper reporter) became a hero thanks to the extraordinary powers he possessed did not seem to have a place on the market at the time. However, in 1938 National Publications was starting a new, ongoing comic book anthology called *Action Comics*, and they were desperate for features. An editor-acquaintance recalls rejecting the comic strip pitch and recommending *Superman* to National. After some changes were made (Siegel and Shuster had to turn their comic strip samples into a thirteen-page comic book story, which required some cutting and pasting), "Superman" was ready to be the lead feature in *Action Comics* #1, and the comic book industry was never the same again.

Superman was soon one of the highest-selling publications in the whole country, selling over a million copies a month, and in no time every comic book company was rushing to put out its own superhero comic book. Siegel and Shuster went from being a pair of unknown teens trying to break into the comics industry to being two of the most famous creators in the United States. Eventually, though, they began to resent the fact that they had sold the rights to their character for only $130, while *Superman* was making National Comics millions of dollars. In 1947 the pair sued National, to recoup their rights to *Superman*, and lost. They were fired from the comic and had their "created by" credit stricken from the books. It was not until the late 1970s, due to public outcry over their treatment during the publicity leading to the release of *Superman: The Movie*, that Siegel and Shuster were given a stipend for the rest of their lives (originally around $35,000 and believed to be more later on), medical benefits, and a "created by" credit from that point forward.

By the time the film was released, Superman had already become an American institution, with comic books, movie serials (both animated and live action), a popular radio series, and a popular television series (not to mention as many licensed products as you could imagine). The film, though, brought a brand-new wave of popularity and went on to spawn three sequels during the 1980s and a relaunch of the film franchise in 2006.

When Siegel and Shuster sold the rights to Superman in 1939, copyrights lasted for only fifty-six years (an initial twenty-eight-year period followed by a twenty-eight-year renewal period). In 1976 the United States Congress passed a new copyright act, which extended the protection period from fifty-six to seventy-five years. In part, the act allowed people (or their heirs) who sold their copyrights to cancel the transfer of their copyright and get it back for the additional nineteen years, under the theory that when they sold the copyright it was only for fifty-six years, so it would be unfair for the buyer to gain the benefit of those extra nineteen years.

Just recently, the heirs of Jerry Siegel (Joe Shuster had no heirs) successfully regained their half of the Superman copyright, giving them one-half of the Superman copyright in the United States (retroactive to 1999). However, in 1998 another new copyright act was passed, this time extending the copyright-protection period from seventy-five to ninety years. This time around, not only can heirs cancel the transfer, but also the estates of the original copyright holders. Therefore, the estate of Joe Shuster will be able to regain his half of the Superman copyright in 2013 (seventy-five years after the publication of *Action Comics* #1) for the extra fifteen years of copyright protection, meaning DC might very well lose the copyright to Superman in only a few short years.

AS YOU MIGHT imagine, Jerry Siegel and Joe Shuster, as two Jewish men from Cleveland, were no fans of the Nazis during World War II, so I am sure they took great pleasure in the offer they received from *Look* magazine in early 1940. *Look* wanted the pair to draw a short story demonstrating how Superman would handle the war in Europe, which was still almost two years away from directly involving the United States.

Their story involves Superman getting fed up with the war, so he flies over to Europe, smacks around the German troops for a little bit, then flies into Hitler's bunker and captures Hitler. Superman then makes a stopover in the Soviet Union, to capture Stalin as well. He then flies the two men to Geneva, for a war-crimes trial before the League of Nations, where both Hitler and Stalin are found guilty of "modern history's greatest crime—unprovoked aggression against defenseless nations." It is particularly interesting to note just how Stalin was viewed at the time, as presumably Siegel's take on Stalin would not be much different from the average American's prior to the uneasy alliance struck up by President Roosevelt and Stalin later in World War II.

While you might imagine that Nazi Germany would not be a fan of this story, you would probably also think that a two-page comic book story would not draw much attention, but surprisingly Siegel and Shuster's tale drew a response from none other than *Das Schwarze Korps*, the official newspaper of the Nazi Schutzstaffel (also

known as the SS—Hitler's elite military force), a month after the story appeared. In the piece, the author decries the story and *Superman* in general (while, interestingly enough, showing a certain amount of admiration for the comic's sheer novelty) as an example of American aggression and for stressing brawn over brains—particularly the simplicity of Superman kidnapping two world leaders and dropping them off at the League of Nations. He further explains how Siegel uses the character to undermine the minds of the youth of America (naturally, there are also more than a few unkind epithets directed toward the Jewish Siegel) by feeding them hate, suspicion, evil, and criminality rather than courage and justice. It's fascinating to see the Nazi propaganda machine so concerned with something as simple as a short superhero story.

DURING THE WAR, the covers of the *Superman* comics prominently displayed advertisements urging the purchase of war bonds and radiated overall pride in the troops "over there," but the comics inside rarely dealt with the war—mostly, I suppose, because of the sheer disjunction of having a superpowerful hero interacting in an all-too-real war. A few stories here and there attempted to explain why Superman was not fighting on the European battlefront, but for the most part, it was simply ignored until, toward the very end of the war, Clark Kent began serving as a war correspondent on a Naval vessel, the USS *Davey Jones*.

Jerry Siegel, though, who was drafted in early 1943, managed to get one dramatic war story into the *Superman* comic strip before departing (drawn by Joe Shuster and a team of assistants because of Shuster's increasingly deteriorating vision, which had kept him from being drafted for military service). And what a story it was! In the monthlong tale, readers marveled as Superman invaded Nazi Germany to rescue no less of a figure than Santa Claus!

The story opens with three leaders of the Axis—German führer Adolf Hitler, Italian premier Benito Mussolini, and Japanese general

Hideki Tōjō—gathered together as Germany's head propagandist, Joseph Goebbels, delivers a message to the people of the world: Santa Claus has been captured by Nazi forces! The readers see the devastation that the news brings all over the world, but they also see Superman quickly make the decision to rescue Santa, even if it means invading Germany.

Along the way, Superman saves the lives of some French resistance fighters, and they aid him in his mission. During his time as a prisoner, Santa Claus gets in a number of speeches explaining how evil the Axis powers are.

© DC Comics, image courtesy of Todd Hillmer

Eventually, Superman rescues Santa Claus and gets him back to the North Pole just in time to help him deliver toys around the world (including an empty gift box for Hitler).

ALMOST SIXTY YEARS later there was another Superman story involving the Nazis, only it went over a bit less successfully. In 1998, in celebration of Superman's sixtieth anniversary, each of the four monthly Superman titles spent a few months telling stories set during different points in Superman's history. For instance, one title told a story that evoked the Superman stories of the 1960s and another told a story that evoked the stories from the 1970s. In the pages of *Superman: The Man of Steel*, the longtime creative partnership of writer Louise Simonson and cowriter/artist Jon Bogdanove unfurled a story set in the 1940s, at the time of the Holocaust.

Bogdanove expertly re-created the style that Joe Shuster used in drawing *Superman* at the time, and the story made clever use of comparing Superman to the traditional Jewish figure of the mystical, superstrong golem, specifically the classic piece of Jewish folklore about Rabbi Judah Loew creating a golem to defend the Prague ghetto from anti-Semitic attacks during the sixteenth century. In the story, Clark Kent is sent to Europe to expose the horrors that were being inflicted by the Nazis. While undercover as a resident of the ghetto, Superman ends up protecting the denizens in much the same way that the famous golem did in the sixteenth century. The story is told with quite a few graphic depictions of the conditions in the ghetto and the savagery of the Nazis. However, many people were put off by the fact that DC Comics made a specific point of telling the whole story without using the words *Jew* or *Holocaust*.

When the story became a bit of an issue (even making it onto the *Howard Stern* morning radio show), the editor of the title, Joey Cavalieri, explained his decision to specifically excise the words in question (together with the word *Catholic*) in an attempt to *avoid* offending anyone. He felt that young readers might end up using the insults the Nazis in the comic hurl at Jewish children and that a comic designed to speak of tolerance shouldn't give more fodder to intolerances. Thus Cavalieri chose to make readers search a bit for the identity of the people that the Nazis were persecuting. Such phrases as the "target population of the Nazis' hate" and the "murdered residents" were used, although a great deal of Yiddish was used as well, so it was not exactly a mystery—just not evident to children unfamiliar with the history of the Holocaust.

DC issued a public apology for the incident, which was accepted by the head of the Jewish Anti-Defamation League.

THESE WERE NOT the only times that DC Comics found the content of its *Superman* comics closely examined by outside forces. In fact, during the 1940s a number of Superman stories drew reactions from the United States Department of War that might lead one to ask the question, "Is Superman a spy?"

The first two instances came from issues of *Superman* that the U.S. government (which kept a watchful eye on popular publications of the time) quietly asked DC to hold off from publishing. The first, "The Battle of the Atoms," was written by Don Cameron, Jerry Siegel's successor as writer of the *Superman* comic when Siegel went to war. In it, Lex Luthor attacks Superman with what Luthor calls "an atomic bomb." It holds no resemblance to an actual atomic bomb, but the government felt it would be better to avoid any mention of the term *atomic bomb* until it was made public that the government was developing one, so the story was delayed for a couple of years.

The second, "Crime Paradise," was written by a writer whose name has been lost to history (credits at the time were nonexistent, but it was most likely Cameron, Alvin Schwartz, or perhaps even Siegel after he returned from the service). "Crime Paradise" was written after the atom bomb became public and was about Superman filming an atom bomb detonation for the army. The comic was again delayed for a year or so, most likely because the government preferred not to have the atom bomb featured in this manner so soon after its use in World War II.

The most notable example, though, was Alvin Schwartz's *Superman* comic strip, which led to the U.S. War Department filing official reports on its attempts to keep Schwartz's story quiet. Schwartz was a young, well-read author who worked in comics for a number of years. He joined Cameron on the comic books but was also the successor to Siegel on the *Superman* comic strip. In 1945 DC Comics was contacted by the War Department over a story Schwartz was developing in the strip that involved a cyclotron (also called an atom smasher), which was what physicists used throughout the 1940s to develop the very first nuclear power plants in America. During that period, all nuclear research was kept under strict government control because of fears that it would lead to other countries developing nuclear weapons. Any possible leaks were cause for concern, so when Schwartz wrote a story involving one of the key tools in current nuclear research, the government sprang into action.

The FBI first approached Siegel in the army, thinking that he was still writing the comic (his byline was still on the strip). When he explained that he was no longer working on the strip, the War Department went directly to DC Comics to ask them to censor the strip, which they did. Later on, the agent assigned to the case, Lt. Col. John Lansdale Jr., explained in a memo his twofold reasons for getting involved with the *Superman* strip. The first, as mentioned above, was fear of a leak, even from a comic strip. The second, and more prominent, reason, though, was that nuclear energy was soon to become an important part of American power, and the government wanted its citizens to take the mechanics of it seriously. They felt this would be undermined if they were appearing as part of *Superman* comics.

Amusingly enough, Alvin Schwartz was informed of the situation when a number of newspapers featured the story after the war (no one told him about the controversy at the time) and revealed where he got his information about the cyclotron: an article he had read in *Popular Mechanics* a decade earlier!

THE NAZIS WERE not the only real-life bad guys that Superman found himself dealing with back in the 1940s. In a memorable story line from the Superman radio series, Superman went head-to-head with the Ku Klux Klan!

The story was the brainchild of the author Stetson Kennedy, who spent a good amount of time after World War II infiltrating the Ku Klux Klan, along with a network of other undercover agents, all working together to get as much information on the secretive racist organization as possible. Kennedy's theory was that if he was to pierce the cloak of secrecy the Klan surrounded its activities with, then the Klan would lose a great deal of its power.

As a means of achieving this goal, Kennedy contacted the popular Superman radio show, *The Adventures of Superman*, which starred Bud Collyer as Superman (and Clark Kent, naturally), and suggested that they do a series on the Klan, with Kennedy providing information he collected (either in person or through one of his operatives) to make the story more realistic. The show agreed, and in June of 1946 began the story line "The Clan of the Fiery Cross," in which Superman encounters the evil Clan of the Fiery Cross (standing in for the Ku Klux Klan). The story used a number of actual passwords from the Georgia branch of the Klan (which was headed by former Imperial Wizard Dr. Samuel Green), though perhaps less secret information was passed on than listeners might recall. The story was spread out over sixteen parts, so the secret information was similarly divvied out. Still, secret Klan information was distributed to the radio audience of the Superman radio show.

That much is undisputed, but what is disputed is exactly what effect the show's story line had upon the Klan or America's view of the Klan. There have been stories told of the Klan attempting to organize a boycott of the radio show on Georgia radio affiliates, but there has been no real proof of any such boycott attempt, and if there was one, it was not successful, since the show continued to be broadcast normally in Georgia. In addition, the story line has been repeatedly credited with spurring a decrease in Klan enrollment, which seems to be a difficult statement to prove, since the Klan did not exactly take a precise census of its membership. Even if there was a decrease, there is yet to be any proof that the decline was related to the Superman series (Klan membership had been dropping steadily since the 1930s).

A PLACE WHERE the Superman radio show did have an undisputed impact was on the Superman mythos as a whole. *The Adventures of Superman* had its radio debut in early 1940, less than two years after the creation of the *Superman* comic book. The show lasted an impressive eleven years, finally coming to an end in March 1951. Until the late 1940s, when it expanded to a thrice-weekly half-hour show, it ran in syndication three to five times a week, in fifteen-minute installments usually airing in the late afternoon or early evening. In an attempt to maintain the illusion that Superman actually appeared on the program, his portrayer, actor Bud Collyer, went uncredited for the first six years of the show's run.

Due to the fact that there were only two years' worth of stories to adapt from the comic book, the radio show quickly ran out of stories and was forced to create some of its own. And the radio show

© Moviehouse Productions

Superman star Bud Collyer reading about the man he portrays on air.

was not always consistent with the comics. In fact, in the second episode the radio show came up with its own origin story that was drastically different from the one in the comics, but this story, which involved Superman coming to Earth as an adult and befriending a professor who helped him take the identity of a reporter named Clark Kent so as to study Earth, did not catch on with the public.

The radio show had better luck with the characters it introduced. If the comic did not have a character it needed, and often even if it did, the radio program just created a new one. A number of these new characters, like Superman's police contact Inspector Henderson, became so popular that they were quickly adapted for use in the comic books. The most notable new additions were Clark Kent's coworkers at the *Daily Planet* (in fact, the radio show came up with the name *Daily Planet*—the comic called it the *Daily Star* in the original stories), specifically editor Perry White and cub reporter Jimmy Olsen. Olsen, in particular, was so popular that he had his own spin-off comic that lasted for over a decade, *Superman's Pal, Jimmy Olsen.*

One of the radio show's strangest additions to the Superman mythos was the introduction of Kryptonite, the pieces of Superman's home planet Krypton that came to Earth in the explosion that destroyed said planet. The small fragments are radioactive and are highly deadly to Superman. The radio show came up with the idea of Kryptonite because of a format constraint. Since it was a weekly program, the writers needed gimmicks to give Collyer opportunities to take vacations. In the episodes with Kryptonite, Superman is deathly ill, so another actor could simply make moaning noises to fill in for Collyer. Kryptonite was soon added to the Superman comics, and over the years many different varieties of Kryptonite have popped up, each one having a different effect on Superman (the most popular varieties are green, which hurts Superman, and red, which causes different unpredictable transformations, like turning him into a dragon or a giant).

WHILE KRYPTONITE MADE its first appearance in the Superman radio show, it could have been in the comics first if it had been up to Jerry Siegel. He wrote a script in 1940 that would have dramatically shifted the Superman mythos but instead ended up dramatically shifting the creative dynamic between him and DC Comics.

"The K-Metal from Krypton," written by Siegel and drawn by Joe Shuster's studio, was most likely originally intended to appear in 1940 in *Superman #8.* In this tale, Siegel introduced K-Metal, a meteor made up of pieces from the exploded Krypton that was passing close to Earth. As it passed by, Superman felt weak and lost his powers. After hearing a scientist explain where the meteor came from, Superman realized for the first time that he was from the planet Krypton (this was not revealed to Superman in the comics for a number of years). Later, while investigating some crooked miners with gangster connections, Clark Kent and reporter/love interest Lois Lane are trapped inside a mine shaft with a group of gangsters, slowly losing oxygen. While there, though, the meteor travels far enough from Earth for its radiation to cease affecting Superman. With his strength returned, he must make a choice—with the group trapped in a small space, there would be no way he could save them without revealing his secret identity.

Ultimately, he decides that their lives are more important than his secret, and so he rescues them all. The gangsters, upon being freed, take the opportunity to attack Superman and Lois, and the end result is an avalanche that kills everyone except Superman and Lois. With the knowledge of his secret identity, a beaming Lois quickly agrees to become Superman's partner, helping him to maintain his secret identity. After some time to reflect, though, her disposition changes: she realizes that Superman/Clark has played her for a fool for years. Still, she agrees to act as his partner, but only for the good of mankind, not because of any personal feelings for him.

The script was drawn and ready for publication when DC editorial coordinator Whitney Ellsworth decided to pull the story (see page 37, where Ellsworth makes a similarly important editorial decision). No specific reason was ever given, but one would think that the dramatic change in the Superman-Lois relationship was the deciding factor. Ellsworth was also the DC liaison to the Superman radio show, so it would not be surprising to learn that he passed on the unpublished Kryptonite idea to the show's writers (although this has never been established). With this decision, it became clear for the first time in the history of the young strip that the destiny of the characters would not be controlled by Superman's creators but by DC Comics.

The story was lost until, almost fifty years later, a DC employee, Mark Waid (who would later go on to become a popular writer for DC), discovered a faded, dusty copy of Siegel's scripts in a box at the back of DC's library archives. While DC has decided not to publish the script, at least fans now have access to the original story. In fact, there is a Web site (http://k-metal.cc) where a group of artists illustrate Siegel's script.

Interestingly enough, in the 1990s DC ended up doing what it would not let Siegel do in 1940: allow Superman to reveal his secret identity to Lois Lane and let the pair eventually become husband and wife.

IN THE 1980S, DC rebooted *Superman*. It brought in a new writer-artist, John Byrne, and gave him the freedom to revamp the entire line of Superman comics. Byrne ended up keeping about 90 percent of the elements of the comic before the reboot, changing only relatively minor aspects of the character. One of the changes was that Clark Kent was given a bit of a makeover and depicted as more of an attractive character in his own right. Indicative of this change in his characterization, the writers that followed Byrne eventually had Lois Lane date Clark Kent. The two became a steady couple, and finally in 1990 Clark proposed to Lois and she accepted! Soon after the engagement was announced, the next big shock came when Clark revealed his secret identity to Lois.

In 1991 the creative teams and editorial staff of the Superman titles (at that point consisting of four different titles) got together to plan the next step in the Superman mythos, which at the time was thought to include the marriage of Clark Kent and Lois Lane. The proposal took place in *Superman (Vol. 2)* #50, so the plan was to have the wedding take place in #75, in late 1992. However, a bit of a snag came from outside DC Comics editorial.

© Warner Bros. Entertainment

As noted earlier, DC Comics is

a subsidiary of Warner Bros. Entertainment, and at the time Warner Bros. was planning a new Superman TV series. It was to focus more on Lois Lane (early possible titles included *Lois Lane's Daily Planet*), and by 1991 the name had changed to *Lois & Clark: The New Adventures of Superman*.

While the series was not scheduled to start until 1993, Warner Bros. felt that the comics should begin taking the television series into consideration before its debut. Since the new series would be very much based on the emerging relationship between Lois and Clark in the comics (which differed from the classic stories where Lois has no interest in Clark as she pines for Superman), it was felt that eventually the characters would get married on the television series, so the comics should hold off until the show got to that point.

With the marriage story taken off the table, the Superman comic creators came up with a crazy idea that ended up being one of the highest-selling comic book stories of all time: instead of marrying Superman off, they would kill him off! "The Death of Superman," in late 1992, caught the public's attention in ways no one could have imagined, and the end result was booming sales for the Superman titles, with total sales in the millions and more media coverage than DC could have possibly expected (especially considering that the death had been announced in advertising months earlier).

Eventually, of course, Superman returned from the dead, and Lois and Clark were back together. However, since their relationship could not end in marriage until the television series (which was doing quite well in the ratings with them being single) got to that point, the writers decided to have Lois and Clark break up in the comics. This happened in early 1996. However, after seeing the ratings for *Lois & Clark* go down, the producers and ABC quickly decided to have Lois and Clark marry early in the 1996–7 season, well ahead of schedule, in hopes of saving the show. So now, with very little notice, the comics had to get Lois and Clark back together and marry them all within a month (see pages 112–14 for a similar problem at Marvel). The marriage, sadly, did not end well for the TV series, which was canceled at the end of the 1996–7 season.

THE SUPERMAN COMICS often had to deal with the fact that adaptations of the character into other media were not always going to be particularly faithful, although occasionally, as with some of the characters created for the radio show, the changes were good enough to be incorporated back into the comics themselves. One such change came about, not as a well-thought-out addition to the mythos, but as a simple attempt at saving money.

Fleischer Studios was an animation house run by two brothers, Max and Dave Fleischer. At the height of its popularity, it was the number one competitor to Walt Disney's cartoons. Before it began working with the Superman character, Fleischer Studios' most notable characters were Betty Boop and Popeye, who both starred in popular theatrical shorts throughout the 1940s. However, the animation world changed dramatically in 1939 with the release of Disney's *Snow White and the Seven Dwarfs*. This high-quality, full-length color movie revolutionized the marketplace for animated theatrical films. Fleischer Studios felt that it needed to respond, so it began hiring more animators and producing full-length features too. These longer films came with larger costs, which were hard for the small studio to bear. Soon Fleischer Studios began looking for ways to cut costs wherever it could.

Even though, to achieve the same high-quality look as the Disney films, Fleischer's 1941 series of *Superman* shorts marked the company's highest budget up to that point (about fifty thousand dollars), it was still important to cut corners wherever possible. One such corner was Superman's method of transportation. *The Adventures of Superman* radio show had a notable tagline, describing Superman as "faster than a speeding bullet, more powerful than a locomotive, and able to leap tall buildings in a single bound." Note the last part: "leap," not fly. In his early appearances, Superman could not fly. He simply jumped large distances (or occasionally ran on power lines). To animate Superman jumping, however, required extra frames to be drawn of Superman crouching down and then leaping upward. A way to avoid drawing these extra frames was to simply take the frame with Superman standing and move it up slowly over the background, which would make it appear as though he was flying off the ground. The *Superman* animated serials were hugely popular (they were even nominated for an Academy Award in 1942), and soon Superman was flying in the comic as well, which he has been doing ever since.

WHILE THE FLEISCHER Studios animated films were a hit, it took a lot longer to see a full-length Superman feature, animated or live action. There were a couple of live-action film serials in the late 1940s and early 1950s, starring Kirk Alyn as Superman, and they got as far as to produce a script for a possible film in the 1950s based on the television series *Adventures of Superman* (which starred George Reeves as Superman). Still, up until the 1970s there had not yet been a full-length Superman feature. That changed when Warner Bros. sold the rights to make the film to father-and-son producer team Alexander and Ilya Salkind in the early 1970s. They began work on the film in 1973, but it was not released until 1978. Part of the reason for the delay was the way they decided to shoot the movie, which also led to a bizarre change to the ending of the first Superman film.

In the early 1970s, the Salkinds had produced two films about the Three Musketeers, directed by Richard Lester: *The Three Musketeers* and *The Four Musketeers*. As a cost-cutting technique, they tried something that had not been done before—they filmed both features at the same time. This cost less than starting up an entirely new production for the second film, and is the same technique used by New Line and Peter Jackson for the popular film trilogy *Lord of the Rings*. The Musketeers films were a box-office success, so the Salkinds decided to do the same with Superman: have director Richard Donner do two movies at once, *Superman: The Movie* and *Superman II*.

However, the Salkinds were not prepared for how long and costly the film production would be, so with 80 percent of the second film completed, they decided to cease production, fearing that the first film would not be successful and the second film would not even happen. Donner obviously took issue with this approach, and he certainly took issue with the next decision the Salkinds made, which was suggested by Lester, who they had brought in as a sort of informal producer. The end of *Superman II* had Superman, played by Christopher Reeve, facing off against three Kryptonian villains. Superman saves the day by traveling back in time, to before the villains escaped, and preventing their escape. The Salkinds decided to take that ending and make it the ending of the first film instead!

Superman: The Movie was a gigantic success, and the Salkinds made Lester the director of the second film, which he produced by adding new scenes to whatever he wanted to use from Donner's production. This included using, at times, a body double for Gene Hackman, who played Lex Luthor in the films but had finished all his scenes before Lester took over. A second major change was the elimination of any scenes with Marlon Brando, who had played Superman's father in the first film. The Salkinds claim the decision to eliminate Brando was strictly a creative one, but it is worth noting that Brando's contract stipulated that he receive 11.75 percent of the film's gross, making it financially prudent to eliminate him.

In 2006, more than two decades after the 1980 release of *Superman II*, Warner Bros. released a newly edited version of *Superman II* that presented the film as Richard Donner had originally envisioned it.

AS STRANGE AS the behind-the-scenes battles involving the first two Superman films were, nothing compares to the bizarre, almost twenty-year journey to produce a new Superman film after the disappointing box office performance, in 1987, of *Superman IV: The Quest for Peace*. In 1993 Warner Bros. finally regained the rights to Superman from the Salkinds (the Salkinds had allowed another production team to option the rights for *Superman IV*). Warner Bros. then hired producer Jon Peters, a successful film producer who got his big break through his connections with Barbra Streisand.

Peters met Streisand because he was her hairdresser, and after the two began dating, they coproduced her 1976 hit film, *A Star Is Born*. Once he established himself, Peters went on to have an impressive career as a film producer, working on such hits as *Caddyshack*, *Flashdance*, *Rain Man*, and most notably (and most likely why he was chosen by Warner Bros.) Tim Burton's two Batman films. Peters's approach to the title character seemed to be more about what he could take from other films than what he could settle on, and the various scripts he developed over the next decade clearly demonstrated this approach. The film was originally going to be based on the popular 1992 "Death of Superman" story line from the comics, so for the first try at a script, screenwriter Jonathan Lemkin told a tale of Superman fighting the villain who had killed him in the comics—the monstrous alien called Doomsday—and dying, but not before his spirit impregnates Lois Lane, who gives birth to a baby who quickly grows up to defeat Doomsday.

In his take on the script, the second writer, Gregory Poirer, used the longtime Superman villain, the brilliant alien Brainiac as the main bad guy. Brainiac creates Doomsday, sends him after Superman, and Doomsday kills him. Another alien (holding a grudge against Brainiac) swoops in, takes Superman's corpse, and revives him, although Superman is forced to use a robotic suit of armor until his powers return.

Director Kevin Smith, who is a noted comic book fan (and has even written comic books for both DC and Marvel), was brought on to tell basically the same story Poirer had written, only with some new, more comedic elements involved. It seemed evident that Peters had a few constants he felt needed to be included: Doomsday, Brainiac, Superman dying, Superman wearing a suit of armor. When speaking of the film, Smith has pointed out some of the elements Peters wanted in the film that Smith felt were bizarre. One such element Peters insisted on was that Superman at one point fight a giant robot spider. It never made it into the film, but it is notable that Peters produced a film a few years later called *Wild Wild West*, which is set in the nineteenth century, yet the main villain uses a giant robot spider.

Wesley Strick, Dan Gilroy, and William Wisher all took turns at writing scripts that resembled the basic scenario Peters required, with Brainiac and Doomsday, and Superman dying and coming back with a suit of armor. Strick created a darker version of the events to suit the director attached at the time, Tim Burton (Nicolas Cage was to star, though eventually both he and Burton took the money they were paid and left the project).

After screenwriter Paul Attanasio took his crack at the formula, and a brief flirtation with the idea of a Batman and Superman film, J. J. Abrams stepped up to the plate with the first script that really broke free of Peters's ideas. It offered a completely revisionist take on Superman, including a Krypton that did not even explode but was instead torn apart by a civil war. As part of the war, Superman's father sent him away to Earth, but once he begins appearing as Superman, enemies of his father from Krypton attack Earth.

Finally, Bryan Singer, hot off his successful turn with the *X-Men* film franchise, signed on to the film, along with enough clout to direct it with his own vision. Although Peters was still an executive producer on the film, the script Singer chose, by Michael Dougherty and Dan Harris (which Singer would later rewrite himself), did not have any of the four elements that Peters originally insisted upon, but instead followed the original Salkind Superman films—specifically the first Superman film directed by Richard Donner—to the letter. Nineteen years after *Superman*

IV was released, Superman returned to the silver screen in 2006 in the aptly titled *Superman Returns*.

THE RESPECT BRYAN Singer afforded Richard Donner was, sadly, not indicative of the way DC Comics treated two comic book legends when it redrew the work of both Jack Kirby and Alex Toth during the 1970s.

Jack Kirby came to DC in 1970 after establishing himself as one of the most popular artists in the entire comic business during the 1960s while working at Marvel (read much more about Kirby in the Marvel section). Offered any book he wanted, Kirby chose to work on *Superman's Pal, Jimmy Olsen*, because it was the only book that did not have a creative team at the time, and Kirby did not want anyone to lose a job because of him. While on the book, Kirby quickly began introducing a series of new characters who would form the foundation of a separate line of comics he would do for DC. These starred the New Gods, characters caught up in an ancient feud between the good people of the planet New Genesis and the evil denizens of Apokolips, headed by the evil Darkseid (pronounced *dark side*).

Kirby had Superman guest star in his *Jimmy Olsen* stories, to establish these New Gods in the DC Universe, but when he did, strangely enough, DC had a different artist redraw Superman's face! Al Plastino, who was a popular Superman artist during the 1950s (and drew the first appearances of Brainiac and Supergirl), was brought in by DC to redraw Kirby's Superman faces to make them appear consistent with the way the hero looked in his own comic book (which was drawn mostly by artist Curt Swan).

This was especially strange because not only did DC make a big

marketing push about bringing Kirby over to draw books for them in his unique style (only to have another artist redraw his work to make it appear less unique), but the artist they chose to make Superman look like the regular books had not worked on those books for years!

As strange as redrawing Kirby's faces may seem, DC at least had the excuse that Kirby's Superman did look different from the Superman that was familiar to most readers. However, they had no such excuse when they did the same with Alex Toth's Superman. Alex Toth was a notable comic book artist during the 1940s, working for different companies in a number of different genres (superheroes, war stories, romances, Westerns, and horror). Eventually, Toth moved into the world of animation, becoming the designer on the *Space Angel* television series. This caught the eye of Hanna-Barbera, which hired him as the main designer for its action series of the 1960s and '70s, including *Space Ghost*, *Birdman and the Galaxy Trio*, and *The Herculoids*. In 1973 he designed the *Super Friends* for Hanna-Barbera, which was its adaptation of the DC Comics super-hero line and became a massively successful cartoon series.

Due to the popularity of the cartoon series, in 1975 DC put out a one-shot comic book tying into the cartoon series. Toth drew the one-shot. However, on Toth's cover, DC replaced his depiction of Superman's face with a drawing by Curt Swan!

Toth's drawing of Superman's face was good enough for the *Super Friends* TV series, but it was not good enough for a *Super Friends* tie-in comic! Years later DC released a poster version of the one-shot cover, and it managed to fix its error decades later by taking a Super-

This is the back cover that DC took Joth's Superman head from to make the current poster "All-Toth."

man head Toth had drawn for the back cover of the one-shot and putting it on Superman's neck for the poster!

SIMILAR FEARS ABOUT how Superman should be portrayed played a role in the destruction of a comic book starring Superman as a young baby.

During the 1990s, DC began doing a series of comics called Elseworlds, which were stories featuring the famous DC characters in different environments or time periods that were not in continuity with the main books. For instance, the very first Elseworld, *Gotham by Gaslight*, is set in the 1880s and tells the story of Jack the Ripper coming to Gotham City to face off against Batman. In 1999 DC released a one-shot collection of short Elseworlds stories. One of the stories, written and drawn by Kyle Baker, was called "Letitia Lerner, Superman's Babysitter" (her initials are an homage to the amount of notable Superman characters with the initials LL, such as Lois Lane, Lex Luthor, and Superman's girlfriends in high school and college, Lana Lang and Lori Lemaris, respectively).

In the comic, Letitia humorously finds herself having a hard time controlling a superstrong baby.

However, DC president Paul Levitz found some of the scenes in the comic offensive, specifically scenes where the infant Superman crawls into a microwave oven and where he sucks milk directly from

Image courtesy of Loren Collins and Scott Morrison

a cow's udder. Although a few thousand copies had already been printed for distribution in the United Kingdom and some other foreign markets, Levitz ordered the remaining printings pulped at a cost in the thousands of dollars.

Although there were only a few thousand copies of the book available, it still managed to win an industry award, the Eisner, in 2000, both for Best Short Story and for Best Writer/Artist: Humor. Eventually, in 2001, DC produced a hardcover book filled with similarly offbeat stories, titled *Bizarro Comics*. The story was included in the volume, which was released as a softcover two years later.

2

BATMAN

atman was introduced about a year after Superman, in the twenty-seventh issue of National Publications' detective anthology, *Detective Comics* (soon National would take Detective Comics as the name of the company, becoming DC Comics). National was looking to add superheroes to every anthology it had, even the ones that had nothing to do with superheroes. So a detective superhero was the right fit for *Detective Comics*, and in the Batman strip (the first strip was drawn by Bob Kane and written by Bill Finger, although only Kane was credited), readers met millionaire Bruce Wayne who secretly solves crimes as the mysterious hero of the night, the Batman.

Batman (along with his young crime-fighting partner, Robin, who was introduced a year later) quickly soared to high sales, becoming the second most popular superhero at the company next to Superman, a spot he would maintain for the next few decades. Superman and Batman were two of the few superhero characters not only to last into the 1950s but to do so with multiple titles! Still, in the 1960s sales were down, and there was even talk about possibly canceling the comic. Luckily for Batman fans, in 1966 the television network ABC began airing the *Batman* television series. Produced by William Dozier, the series was played for camp laughs, but it was still such a massive success that comic book sales soared once again.

After the television series ended, the comics tried to get back to the darker roots of the Batman character. In the mid-1980s writer-artist Frank Miller created the limited series *Batman: The Dark Knight Returns*, bringing a much darker approach to the character that was notable both for forming a template that the other Batman titles of the day would soon follow and for inspiring Tim Burton to direct the massively successful *Batman* film in 1989.

In the 1990s, on top of a number of popular films (although the film series stalled after its third sequel), Fox launched a popular animated series by acclaimed animation producers Bruce Timm and Paul Dini. *Batman: The Animated Series* was one of the most popular and critically acclaimed animated series of all time and has spun off a number of follow-up Batman (and other DC Comic heroes as well) cartoon series.

Recently, inspired by a different Frank Miller comic book (*Batman: Year One*, which examined the beginning of Batman's career), Warner Bros. launched a new Batman film starting from that origin, titled *Batman Begins*. It was a huge success, spawning a 2008 sequel, *The Dark Knight*.

AS NOTED EARLIER, the only credit on the first Batman comic story was the byline of Bob Kane. Currently, Bob Kane is the sole acknowledged creator of Batman. All Batman comics carry with them the byline at the beginning of the issue, "Batman created by Bob Kane." However, the actual creation of Batman is a good deal more complicated than simply "created by Bob Kane," although it may depend on what one considers the actual creation of the character.

In 1939 National Publications sent a simple plea out to all of its comic creators—give us another Superman! It was with this in mind that Kane, who had created a few series for different publishers in a variety of styles, from funny animals ("Peter Pupp") to an adventure series ("Rusty and His Pals"), began brainstorming to find a new hero to rival Superman. He came up with an idea, and after putting together some designs of the new character, he introduced the Bat-Man to his studio mate, Bill Finger (Finger was an aspiring writer who Kane had recently hired to write some strips).

As both Finger and Kane recalled, the early vision of Bat-Man was a man wearing a red bodysuit, with black wings attached to his back, and a domino mask (similar to the one Robin wore). Finger suggested that they make the suit less colorful by turning the red to gray. He then suggested making the domino mask a bat-shaped cowl, that the hero should wear gloves, and that the wings should be replaced by a cape. Finger then wrote the story that would appear in *Detective Comics* #27, including naming Bruce Wayne and Commissioner Gordon, who both first appeared in that story. So, who created Batman?

Kane quickly signed a twenty-year contract to produce Batman stories for National, a deal he would later renegotiate in the late 1940s when Jerry Siegel and Joe Shuster first sued for the rights to Superman. Part of the deal was that all Batman strips would carry a Bob Kane byline and that Kane would be hired to produce a certain number of Batman stories. DC ultimately bought Kane out of the production deal in the late 1960s.

WHEN IT IS said that Kane was hired to produce a certain amount of Batman stories, it does not mean that Kane himself drew them. Kane was not a particularly proficient artist, and modern comic historians have demonstrated that Kane's original Batman stories were to a great extent produced by using poses and arrangements of other comic artists, including Hal Foster (artist of the popular *Tarzan* comic strip). This was not an unusual occurrence, of course, as most comic book artists of the time swiped from one another. However, once Kane had his deal in place to produce Batman stories, he began to hire other artists to help produce his artwork, and in 1943 he left the comic book entirely to devote his time to the *Batman* comic strip. In

1946 he returned to the comic book, but for the rest of his career as a comic book artist, he was not doing any of the actual art, choosing instead to have other artists ghost draw for him (Lew S. Schwartz from 1946 to 1953 and Sheldon Moldoff from 1953 to 1967). As you can imagine, with so many different people working on the comic, it is extremely difficult to determine who created what—this is never more evident than in the case of Batman's greatest enemy, the Joker.

The most prominent of Kane's early assistants was Jerry Robinson, who was studying to be a journalist when Kane hired him, first to assist with lettering and background inks, until eventually, when Kane stopped drawing the comic in 1943, Robinson became the primary Batman artist (along with Dick Sprang). In 1940, while working for Kane, Robinson brought to work a drawing of a playing card featuring the Joker. The dispute comes about due to a disagreement about when Robinson brought in the card (which was recently loaned by Robinson to the Jewish Museum in New York City for a comic book exhibit). According to Robinson, he showed Kane the card and said they should create a villain based on it. According to Kane, the Joker had already been created when Robinson showed him the card. Kane noted that after he came up with the basic idea

of a villain called the Joker, Bill Finger thought of Conrad Veidt's character in the 1928 silent film *The Man Who Laughs* (about a man punished by being disfigured so that his face is in a perpetual grin), and suggested that that is how the Joker should appear (and with his white makeup, the grinning Joker did end up being based visually on Veidt's character).

What makes this story different from other Kane stories is that this time Finger told a DC editor that he felt Kane's version was correct. Robinson feels that Finger is simply confused about the time frame, and that the Veidt comparison came about after Robinson showed the drawing, but it is likely something that will never be sorted out for certain.

THE WHOLE DEBATE over the Joker's creation might have been made moot if not for the actions of a DC editor. The Joker debuted in the first issue of a brand-new Batman title, *Batman*, in 1940. In the same issue, Catwoman also makes her first appearance—awkward as it is that such a notable creation should make her debut as second fiddle (sort of like how Lois Lane's first appearance is overshadowed by that fellow with the *S* on his shirt).

At the time of *Batman* #1, Bill Finger was still handling most of the writing (although Gardner Fox also wrote some of the early stories), and Finger was not one for recurring villains. If you went up against the Batman, odds were you were going to end up dying in some manner at the end of the issue. The Joker managed to avoid this fate at the end of his first appearance, which was the lead story of *Batman* #1. In the tale, the Joker announces on the radio that he is going to kill a number of notable figures, and he keeps his promise, leaving it to Batman and Robin to stop him. They do so, and he is sent to jail. He returns to fight Batman later in that same issue, in the appropriately titled "The Joker Returns." In that story the Joker escapes from prison and goes on a spree of jewel robberies. Batman sets a trap for him, and the Joker falls right into it. The two men fight each other, and during the struggle the Joker accidentally stabs himself with his own knife and dies at the end of the story.

Luckily for the Joker, he had an unforeseen benefactor. *Batman* editor Whitney Ellsworth (remember him from page 18?) felt that it would be a waste to kill off the character so soon, so he actually had them add an extra panel to the issue, after the comic was otherwise completed, in which an ambulance driver remarks something along the lines of, "My goodness! He's still alive!" The Joker would go on to become almost as famous as Batman himself.

ONE REASON THAT there were so few recurring characters in the early days of the Batman comics is that the stories were a good deal bloodier than they later became. In fact, for the first year or so of his existence Batman routinely used a gun!

Even without the gun, Batman was not a particularly pleasant fellow. In his very first appearance, in *Detective Comics* #27, Batman breaks a thug's neck with a kick and also punches a villain off a catwalk and into a vat of acid, declaring that the villain's gruesome death was "a fitting end to his kind." Over the next year, Batman would break at least four more necks, and even after Robin joined him as his partner Batman kept up the killing, most notably in *Detective Comics* #39, in which Batman fights a Chinese gang called the Tong of the Green Dragon. During one fight, Batman intentionally topples an idol onto the bad guys, killing six members of the gang!

While to find Batman killing at all is odd, it is especially strange to see him bearing arms, but that's what he did in *Detective Comics* #32, in which he uses a gun that fires silver bullets to kill a vampire. The next time Batman used a gun, editor Whitney Ellsworth stepped in once again.

In the second story of the aforementioned *Batman* #1, Batman faces off against the evil mad scientist Hugo Strange, who has developed a growth hormone that can turn normal men into monsters. While in his Batplane, Batman spies the truck carrying the monster

© DC Comics

men, and while he regrets doing it, he decides to use the machine gun mounted on his plane to riddle the monster men with bullets.

Ellsworth declared that Batman should never intentionally kill again, and he didn't. In an amusing emphasis of this point, a few issues later Batman picks up a discarded gun and uses it to wing a bad guy. An editor's note explains: "The Batman never carries nor kills with a gun!"

SOON BATMAN AND Robin were so popular that they even gained, in 1941, their own shared title with Superman, *World's Finest Comics*. It had its origins in a special World's Fair comic starring Superman, which National Publications put out in 1939 (this was before Batman was introduced). For the 1939–40 World's Fair, DC also did a second one-shot comic, this time featuring Batman and Superman stories. The comic was such a success that they launched *World's Finest Comics* (the first issue was called *World's Best Comics* but was retitled with #2). The comic was originally a quarterly that featured stories with a variety of DC superheroes and always included Batman and Superman. The two heroes appeared on the covers together, but they never appeared together in the stories— there would be one Superman story and one Batman story.

The heroes finally met each other in a comic (discounting their work with the Justice Society of America, which featured a number of other heroes too) in 1952 in *Superman* #76. Interestingly enough, the two met on the radio show a number of years earlier, in another one of the episodes designed to give Superman actor Bud Collyer time off (Batman and Robin would fill in for Superman). Still, *World's Finest* continued to offer two separate stories until *World's Finest Comics* #71, in 1954. The reason DC decided to team up the heroes was a simple one—inflation!

Back in the 1940s and 1950s, comics dealt with inflation differently. Rather than raise prices, what publishers did was to reduce the *size* of the comic, in both its dimensions and the number of pages. For instance, *World's Finest Comics* was one hundred pages long through #9, ninety-two pages long through #12, eighty-four pages long through #18, seventy-six pages long through #54, and sixty-eight pages long through #70. At the same time, the height and width of the comic slowly shrunk as well.

With #71, the book made its biggest jump, from sixty-eight pages to thirty-six. At this point, it did not have *room* for both a Superman and a Batman story, so instead they decided to team the two heroes up, and that was the way the book continued (except for a short period when *World's Finest Comics* became a team-up book between Superman and various heroes) until the series finally ended in 1986, right before John Byrne's Superman revamp. In 2003 DC brought its team-up book back; titled simply *Superman/Batman*, it has been one of DC's highest-selling titles since its debut.

* * *

WHILE THERE HAVE been a number of stylistic changes over the years, the appearance of Batman has been remarkably consistent over almost seventy years. Perhaps the most notable change to the character happened when editor Julius "Julie" Schwartz took over the Batman titles in 1964. Schwartz was the editor behind the resurgence of superheroes at DC Comics in the late 1950s, with the introduction of new superheroes based on the heroes of the 1940s, such as the Flash, Green Lantern, Hawkman, and the Atom. Due to his success on these titles, DC assigned him the Batman titles, which were in a bit of a sales lull at the time.

Schwartz brought with him Carmine Infantino, who had been the artist on the Flash revamp. With their first issues, they introduced a new costume for Batman. For the first twenty-plus years of his existence, Batman's chest insignia was a simple black bat on his gray chest. With Batman's "new look", the black bat was placed on top of a yellow oval.

Many theories have been proposed as to why DC chose to give Batman the yellow oval, the most popular being that DC wished to have a logo that it could trademark. You cannot trademark a simple depiction of a bat—it would be considered too common—but you could trademark a drawing of a bat on a yellow oval. While this is an interesting take on trademark law, it also has no basis in actual law, as the stylized Batman chest insignia is clearly unique enough to be considered a trademark. The drawing of the bat alone was already quite stylized.

That said, whether the Batman chest insignia would have been available for trademark without the yellow oval or not, Julie Schwartz has explained many times in the past that that was not under consideration when they made the move. Rather, it was an attempt to distinguish the new take on Batman from the stories that preceded it. Later, producer William Dozier would credit the Infantino visual redesign as a major factor in his choosing to do the *Batman* television series. (In an interesting turn of events, the television series was almost made using the original insignia—the first Batman costumes had the old insignias on them, but they were replaced with the new yellow oval ones just before the show began filming.)

The yellow logo became a long-standing part of Batman's costume, although more recent artists felt that the bright yellow oval in the middle of his chest took away from Batman's "creature of the night" appearance. While he was forced to use the yellow oval in his *The Dark Knight Returns* miniseries in 1986, Frank Miller first explained why Batman wore such a bright oval: it was where he carried heavy bulletproof armor, so he was essentially giving crooks a target where he was most protected—one that would draw them away so they would not shoot him where he was more exposed. Miller then demonstrated the effectiveness of this target by having someone shoot Batman in the yellow oval, and when Batman got his costume fixed later in the series, Miller surreptitiously dropped the yellow oval for the rest of the series. Eventually, in 2000, DC followed Miller's lead and dropped the yellow oval from Batman's costume in the comics, and it has not been used since (the current Batman film series also does not use it).

THE *BATMAN* TELEVISION series was one of the most notable comic-book-related pieces of pop culture to come into existence since comic books began. The influence it had was considerable, although that influence has also been overstated at times. One such overstatement involves the creation of the character Aunt Harriet Cooper, played by Madge Blake on the television series for three years. The creation of Aunt Harriet has often been attributed to the Dozier television series, but Aunt Harriet appeared in the comics a good two years before she was used on the show.

The genesis of the Aunt Harriet character (the maternal aunt of Dick Grayson, also known as Robin, who came to live with Bruce Wayne and Dick at stately Wayne Manor) took place for much the same reasons that Bob Kane and Sheldon Moldoff created Batwoman in 1957 (and later, Bat-Girl in 1961). For years, people had made crude jokes about the relationship between Batman and Robin. However, in 1954, when psychiatrist Dr. Fredric Wertham began his campaign against comics with the publication of *Seduction of the Innocent*, which ultimately led to a congressional hearing about the effects comic books had among children, he made a point of stating that Batman and Robin's relationship, living together alone in a mansion, appeared to be a homosexual one. Quickly, Kane and Moldoff (who was ghosting for Kane at the time) introduced Batwoman as a love interest for Batman and, a few years later, Bat-Girl as a love interest for Robin.

When Schwartz took over the title, he did not like Batwoman or Bat-Girl, but he did think there was something to be said for deemphasizing Batman and Robin's close living quarters. He felt that a way to avoid such an interpretation was to add a female to the cast living in Wayne Manor. So Schwartz had Batman's loyal butler, Alfred Pennyworth, killed off and brought in Aunt Harriet to replace him.

While Dozier liked the addition of Aunt Harriet, when he read the first script for the new series, he noted that there was no Alfred in the show. When he was informed that they had killed him off, Dozier was displeased and demanded that Alfred be brought back. If he was going to be in the series, Schwartz felt he should be in the comic as well, so Schwartz had to find a way to bring Alfred back to the comic, and fast, with the end result being trouble for Batman writer Gardner Fox.

When Fox got rid of Alfred in the comic, it was in a fairly direct manner. In *Detective Comics* #328 from 1964, Alfred pushes Batman and Robin out of the way of a boulder, which ends up killing him. It is fairly difficult to bring back an ordinary human from being crushed by a boulder, especially when the resurrection has to occur promptly. So what Schwartz had the Batman creative team do was to take a story line that had been going on for a while and abruptly make it about Alfred's return.

For a number of months, a mysterious villain known only as the Outsider had been terrorizing Batman through various intermediaries. In *Detective Comics* #356 from 1966 (right around the time the *Batman* television series debuted), the identity of the Outsider is revealed—and it's Alfred! Apparently, a scientist had taken Alfred's body and attempted a regeneration experiment on the corpse, the resulting regeneration made Alfred appear like a monster. He also gained superpowers and an overwhelming desire to kill Batman and Robin, not to mention a disdain for humanity as a whole—he felt "outside" of humanity, hence the name.

At the end of the issue, Batman manages to reverse the effects of the regeneration, and Alfred is back to his usual self. Everything went back to the status quo, just in time for the television series.

Of course, what happened was that Schwartz had writer Gardner Fox change the original identity of the Outsider (whom exactly Fox originally wanted the Outsider to be is still a mystery) and make him Alfred, so that he could quickly get Alfred back into the comics to appease Dozier.

IN SEPTEMBER 1967, in the beginning of the third season of the *Batman* television series, Yvonne Craig joined the cast as Batgirl. Although she first appeared in the comics in early 1967, Batgirl's origins are inexorably wrapped up in the *Batman* television series.

As mentioned before, there had been a Batgirl in the comics before (or rather, a Bat-Girl), but she had disappeared when Schwartz took over the titles. When the *Batman* television series began, though, Carmine Infantino immediately thought about what effect the television series might have on the comic book. Schwartz was thinking this too, so he asked Infantino to work on improving the supporting cast of the *Batman* title, specifically with characters that could be used for the television show and even more specifically female characters, which the Batman books had a shortage of, save Catwoman.

Infantino's first creation was the villainous Poison Ivy, a plant-themed villain, who debuted in 1966, in *Batman* #181.

Poison Ivy never made her way on to the television show, but she became one of the more notable Batman villains on the animated series in the early 1990s and ultimately became one of the main villains of the third Batman film sequel, *Batman & Robin*, in 1997.

When Dozier was attempting to secure a third season of the *Batman* series from ABC, he asked Schwartz if they had any female characters that he could take to the network with as a promise for the show. Schwartz gave Dozier some designs Infantino had done for a new Batgirl, which Dozier

brought to the network, who liked the idea enough to approve a third season of the series, with Batgirl to play a prominent role. The next step was to actually introduce the character, which Infantino and Gardner Fox did in *Detective Comics* #359. They decided to make the new Batgirl noticeably different from Kane and Moldoff's Bat-Girl, who was more a hanger-on than an independent character. The new Batgirl was Barbara Gordon, the young-adult daughter of Commissioner Gordon, who worked as a li-

brarian by day and a crime fighter by night. Batgirl was soon popular enough to appear regularly over the next two decades, and Yvonne Craig certainly made an impression on many viewers with her one season portraying young Ms. Gordon.

WHILE BATGIRL WAS a popular supporting cast member for a number of years, by the 1980s she began to become a less important figure in the Bat titles. Additionally, as noted earlier, during the mid-to-late 1980s, the influence of Frank Miller's work on Batman led to much darker comic book stories, where there was not as much room for a librarian fighting crime in high heels (although, by the mid-1980s, Barbara Gordon had actually been elected to Congress!).

In 1984 artist Brian Bolland was putting the finishing touches on an acclaimed maxi-series he had created with writer Mike W. Barr, *Camelot 3000*, which was about King Arthur and the Knights of the Round Table being reincarnated in the future to save the earth from alien invasion. With that title ending, Bolland literally had his pick of any project he wanted to do at DC. He decided that he wanted to work on a Batman one-shot with writer Alan Moore, a fellow British comic creator who had recently begun working for DC writing the title *Swamp Thing*, turning that book into one of the most critically acclaimed comics of the decade.

The resulting work took Bolland a few years to draw (as a particularly detailed artist, Bolland works fairly slowly, which is why he mostly just draws comic book covers these days), but when it was finally released in 1988, *Batman: The Killing Joke* became very likely the second most influential Batman work next to Frank Miller's comics.

© DC Comics

It was an inspired look into the madness behind Batman's greatest villain, the Joker. However, a character that did not fare so well was Barbara Gordon, Batgirl. In the comic, the Joker comes to visit Gordon and her father, the police commissioner (and Batman's longtime ally) James Gordon, and when she answers the door, Joker shoots her in the stomach, paralyzing her from the waist down. He then proceeds to kidnap and torture her father.

While this dark work was highly influential (the late Heath Ledger was given a copy of the book to study for his portrayal of the Joker in the *Batman Begins* sequel, *The Dark Knight*), some wondered whether DC really intended to have Batgirl crippled—it seemed a bit over the top. However, not only did the book gain editorial approval, earlier in 1988 DC even hired the last writer to handle Batgirl regularly, Barbara Kesel (who wrote her story when Batgirl was a backup feature in one of the Batman titles), to write a one-shot special where she would wrap up any remaining Batgirl story lines and have Barbara retire at the end of the issue, simply to put the character into place for Moore's work. DC definitely intended for this work to "count."

Many readers felt the violence toward Gordon was too much, and even Moore, in retrospect, has expressed his displeasure with how the story turned out. Two writers who were particularly upset were John Ostrander and his wife, Kim Yale. Ostrander was writing a couple of titles for DC at the time, and when he and Yale read *The Killing Joke*, they were dismayed at how Barbara Gordon was treated. They then set out to "fix" the character, as Ostrander slowly introduced Gordon, now a wheelchair-bound computer expert, into *Suicide Squad*, one of the titles he was writing.

This new take on Gordon, now calling herself Oracle, soon became a popular DC character; more popular, in fact, than she was when she was Batgirl. She even gained her own title, *Birds of Prey*, about her and a group of superhero operatives she organizes (sort of like Charlie's

Angels). *Birds of Prey* was even popular enough to spawn a short-lived television show based on the series. So while Barbara Gordon's character was for a time heading somewhere rather dark, her story turned out quite hopeful in the end, thanks to Ostrander and Yale.

As mentioned, the *Batman* television series was extremely popular and resonant in the popular culture, but few people would have expected the effect it had on a certain group of dolphins at Disney's Epcot Center in Florida, who were trained by scientists to sing the theme song to the series!

In 2005 the researchers successfully established that dolphins could not only recognize rhythms but then reproduce them. They began the study by taking each dolphin separately and continually playing it six different short rhythms through an underwater sound projector called a hydrophone. They trained the dolphins to associate each rhythm with a certain action, so that when they played one rhythm, the dolphin would toss a ball, and for another the dolphin would wave its fin.

Once they established that the dolphins were actually differentiating between the various rhythms, they then used positive reinforcement to get the dolphins to repeat rhythms vocally on demand. They would show the dolphins a Batman doll and then reward it with a fish.

Soon, with all the dolphins properly trained, they brought them together to produce the rhythms on presentation of the Batman doll. The result was what appeared to be a group of dolphins singing the *Batman* theme (written by Neal Hefti for the 1966 series), specifically the part that goes "Batman! Batmaaaan! Batmaaaaaaan!" Batman is lucky that the dolphins are friendly; he already has enough aquatic trouble with the Penguin!

SPEAKING OF THE Penguin, while the Batman comics and television series have had a widespread and mostly positive effect on the world, that particular villain may very well have been influential in creating a new way to assassinate people!

Oswald Chesterfield Cobblepot, a short, ugly looking man, gained the nickname the Penguin when he was a child, because of his strange appearance and his love for birds. First appearing in 1941, in *Detective Comics* #58, the Penguin would dress up in fine suits and a top hat, and carry a fancy umbrella, pretending to be the gentleman that he never could be. The umbrellas were his gimmick: he carried a number of different high-tech models with different specialties (one might contain a gun, and others might shoot out poisonous gas, or conceal a blade, etc.). This made for a memorable recurring villain, and the Penguin gained even more fame when he was portrayed on the *Batman* television series by Burgess Meredith, who would waddle and make a squawking noise. Meredith's take on the Penguin made the character one of the show's most popular villains. Danny DeVito would later take on the role in the 1992 film sequel *Batman Returns*. The character was memorable enough, apparently, to inspire a murder that took place in 1978 using an actual high-tech umbrella!

Georgi Markov was a Bulgarian novelist and playwright who was popular during the 1960s. He was also quite critical of Communism, which led to his plays being banned in Bulgaria, a Communist country at the time. In the late 1960s, Markov emigrated to Western Europe and ultimately settled in England, working at the Bulgarian desk of the BBC World Service and continuing to speak out against Communism. The Bulgarian secret police, Darzhavna Sigurnost, likely with assistance from the Soviet Union's KGB, made a number of attempts to kill Markov, finally succeeding in 1978.

Markov says that while waiting at a bus stop by Waterloo Bridge, he was jabbed in the calf by a man carrying an umbrella. By the time he arrived at work, he had developed a large red pimple where the man had jabbed him, and the pain persisted. He developed a high fever, was admitted to the hospital that night, and died three days later.

After his death, an autopsy was performed, and a small metal pellet was found in his calf. The pellet contained two tiny holes, and inside them there were traces of the toxin ricin. The holes had originally been coated with a sugary substance that was designed to melt at 37°C (the temperature of the human body). Once the ricin entered Markov's bloodstream, he was a dead man, as there was not then, nor is there now, a cure for ricin poisoning. The pellet had been fired from a trigger in the top of the umbrella, just like one of Penguin's umbrella devices; a tragic case of life (perhaps) imitating art.

3

DC Comics Miscellanea

A s detailed earlier, Major Malcolm Wheeler-Nicholson was the driving force behind the creation of what eventually became DC Comics, but Wheeler-Nicholson was even more influential than that, as he was one of the first persons to create a comic book containing original content rather than reprinted material. Wheeler-Nicholson was inspired to get into the business by the success of *Famous Funnies*, a series that contained reprints of newspaper comic strips, and in 1934 formed National Allied Publications to publish *New Fun: The Big Comic Magazine* #1, which included comic strip reprints but also a number of original comics, mostly in the funny animal vein. The new venture was not a highly profitable one at the time, as retailers were wary about selling the new product that Wheeler-Nicholson was peddling.

By 1937 Wheeler-Nicholson was deep into debt to Harry Donenfeld, who ran the printing plant that produced Wheeler-Nicholson's comics line (which had expanded to a second title, *New Comics*—later titled *Adventure Comics*), so Wheeler-Nicholson was compelled to take on Donenfeld as a partner for the publication of the next title, *Detective Comics*. A year later, though sales were doing reasonably well on the three titles, Wheeler-Nicholson was still in debt, and Donenfeld took advantage of that debt to force him out of the company, by suing him for nonpayment on the printing fees. This maneuver led to a settlement and Wheeler-Nicholson's departure. He left just before the launch of the fourth title in the line, which happened to be the fairly important *Action Comics* #1.

Taking on forces larger than himself was nothing new to Wheeler-Nicholson, though. During his time in the army, he did no less than take on the entire United States military, ruining his career in the process. Wheeler-Nicholson was a cavalry officer during World War I, but after the war, he was extremely critical of the U.S. Army. Dissatisfied with how the war was handled by the military, and what he felt was the advancement of officers based on nepotism and cliques, in 1922 Wheeler-Nicholson went over the heads of his superiors and sent a letter directly to President Warren Harding, along with a copy to the *New York Times*.

The U.S. War Department answered in the *New York Times*, as well, and the *Times* gave Wheeler-Nicholson a chance to respond, which he did, detailing the areas in which he felt the military was lacking. After a series of hearings, the affair ended with Wheeler-Nicholson's military discharge, at which point he began using his military knowledge as a gimmick in writing war and adventures stories for pulp magazines. While at the pulps, he came up with the idea to do an original comic book series, and when Donenfeld ended that endeavor, Wheeler-Nicholson simply went back to his war stories and military critiques—once you have been in a fight with the U.S. military, publishing battles likely seem mundane.

WHEELER-NICHOLSON HAD BEEN gone from the company for almost two years by the time the Justice Society of America was formed, in 1940, in the pages of *All Star Comics* #3. The group represented the first time a team of established superheroes was formed. What is bizarre about the formation of the team, though, is that the heroes were all from different comic book companies!

As noted earlier, in the early 1940s DC Comics was really a partnership of two companies, National Comics (made up of Donenfeld's Detective Comics and National Publications, which he took from Wheeler-Nicholson) and All-American Comics (Max Gaines's company), which published under the same banner. In fact for a time, in 1944, before Gaines let Donenfeld buy him out (at which point Gaines started his own company, EC Comics—more on that later), All-American Comics even had its own separate logo. So the Justice Society of America in *All Star Comics* #3—which featured the Flash, Hawkman, the Sandman, the Atom, the Spectre, Dr. Fate, Green Lantern, and Hour-Man—was made up of characters who did not even belong to the same company!

The team consisted of characters from four different comic anthologies, two heroes from each anthology. The heroes from Gaines's company were Green Lantern and the Atom from *All-American Comics*, and the Flash and Hawkman from *Flash Comics*. Dr. Fate and the Spectre came from National's *More Fun Comics*, while Hour-Man and the Sandman were from National's *Adventure Comics*.

The other intriguing aspect of the formation of the first supergroup in *All Star Comics* #3 is that its members were not even intended to be a team when the comic was originally produced. As you can tell by the number, this was not the beginning of *All Star Comics*. The first two issues of *All Star Comics* were basically a sampler of the four superhero anthologies produced by National and All-American Publications; the book featured two stories from each of the four anthologies. The editor of the title, Sheldon Mayer, however, came up with a winning idea: give the book more of a hook than just "here are eight short stories."

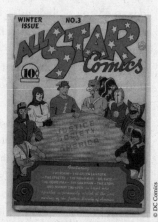

© DC Comics

And that hook was that the heroes were all on a brand-new team together. The issue was originally written as eight solo stories, but Mayer had writer Gardner Fox write a framing sequence that had the heroes form a superhero team, forcing Fox to then come up with a way to tie each short story into the framing sequence (as seen on page 43, Fox has been given some tough assignments).

As a final and interesting twist to the story, Fox has always been credited with writing each of the short stories in the issue, and that's what he himself has claimed. However, if they were initially written to be solo stories, as Fox himself has noted they were, then wouldn't they have been written by each character's regular writer, like they were in the first two issues? Since Fox passed away over twenty years ago, it's unlikely we will ever have a definitive answer to that question.

THOUGH A FOUNDING member of the Justice Society of America, Green Lantern did not have a particularly dignified end to his career as a lead character. Created by Martin Nodell, Green Lantern made his debut in 1940 in *All-American Comics* #16. The story featured Alan Scott, a railroad engineer who discovered an ancient green-metal lantern. In it, a magical green flame appeared and told him how to fashion a ring from the metal of the lantern. When he did so, wearing the ring afforded him a series of wonderful powers, like the ability to fly, walk through walls, zap people with energy blasts, and create solid objects out of thin air. In an interesting idea for a costume, Green Lantern wore an outfit composed of a purple cape, red shirt, and green pants. This odd combination of colors was actually justified in the comic—Scott felt the costume would be so garish that it would frighten criminals!

Green Lantern soon became popular enough that he was given his own ongoing series in 1941. Like most other heroes, Green Lantern eventually gained a sidekick, though his sidekick was a bit different from those of other heroes. More of an assistant, his was a cab

driver named Doiby Dickles (Doiby is
actually Derby, just spoken through a
thick Brooklyn accent), who would often assist by hitting crooks in the
head with a pipe wrench he carried
around with him at all times.

After World War II, superheroes as
a whole fell on hard times, and Green
Lantern felt the sting just like the others. Always looking for a new hook,
the editor of *Green Lantern*, Sheldon
Mayer, felt they should attempt to cash
in on the series of popular dog charac-
ters in radio and film, like Rin Tin Tin and Lassie, so in *Green Lantern*
#30, in 1948, the superhero gained a dog sidekick, Streak the Won-
der Dog. (A few years later, in 1955, "give characters a dog" had a
comeback, as Batman would gain Ace the Bat-Hound and Superman
would meet Krypto the Superdog.) Streak was a big hit with fans, so
much so that soon he became more popular than Green Lantern
himself! For three of the last five issues of *Green Lantern*, including
the final issue, Green Lantern did not appear on the cover of his own
comic—that honor belonged to Streak!

After *Green Lantern* was canceled in 1949 (the concept was re-
vived in 1959 with a new Green Lantern character, this time a member of an intergalactic peacekeeping corps, all of whom had magic
green rings), Streak the Wonder Dog was eventually revamped and
given a new name and his own title in 1952, *The Adventures of Rex the
Wonder Dog*.

WILLIAM MOULTON MARSTON was a noted psychologist who, during
the early 1940s, wrote about the positive effects he felt comic books
had on children (see pages 42 and 67–69 for what the counterar-
gument did to comics). Seeing the industry dominated by male

heroes, though, his wife suggested that he create a female super-hero. He pitched the idea to Max Gaines at All-American Publications. Gaines liked the idea too, and Wonder Woman made her debut in 1941, in *All Star Comics #8*.

Wonder Woman was Princess Diana, a representative of the all-female tribe of Amazons on Paradise Island, who won a contest to be the tribe's representative in "man's world" and help fight the Nazis. Armed with strength, silver bracelets that could deflect bullets, and a golden lasso that could compel anyone encircled by it to tell the truth, Wonder Woman made a formidable hero and is the only character other than Batman and Superman to have had her own title since 1944. What's most striking about her magic lasso is that Marston was actually the inventor of the first modern lie-detector test (which remains an important component of the current polygraph lie-detector test)!

In 1921 Martson published an article based on his doctoral thesis for Harvard University, which discussed the lie-detector test he had developed four years earlier. The title was "Systolic blood pressure symptoms of deception and constituent mental states," and that was Marston's innovation: the idea that by testing a subject's systolic blood pressure one would be able to determine whether the subject was lying. Dr. John A. Larson and Sir James Mackenzie also developed work in the field, and Larson's former assistant, Leonarde Keeler, was the one who successfully combined all of their various work into one device that measured systolic blood pressure, heart rate, respiration, and skin conductivity. This is the device that is used today (although improved upon over the years).

Still, while he may not have created the polygraph test, the inventor of Wonder Woman's lasso of truth did play a significant part in its origin!

ONE THING THAT Harry Donenfeld made a priority at National/DC Comics during his tenure there was that the company would use the law to protect its rights as much as it could. This was especially important following the explosion in popularity that followed Superman's introduction in 1938. Suddenly, new comic book companies were starting up left and right, each coming up with its own version of Superman (for one such instance, see pages 217–18). During this time, none of these heroes challenged the sales or popularity of Superman; that is, until Fawcett Comics introduced Captain Marvel, which is why DC Comics fought over the character for years.

Captain Marvel first appeared in 1940, in *Whiz Comics* #2. He was the most notable character from Fawcett Publications, a pulp magazine publisher that decided to get into comic books in 1939 after seeing the twin successes of Superman and Batman for DC Comics. Writer Bill Parker and artist C. C. Beck created the character, which had an especially novel hook—a young child named Billy Batson, working as a news reporter, was chosen by a wizard named Shazam to be a force for justice. When Billy says the word *Shazam* (an acronym for six historical figures who would give Billy their power: the wisdom of Solomon, the strength of Hercules, the stamina of Atlas, the power of Zeus, the courage of Achilles, and the speed of Mercury) he would transform into Captain Marvel, the World's Mightiest Mortal.

Captain Marvel's powers were similar to Superman's, and he soon became tremendously popular, spinning off a number of related series, including *Captain Marvel Adventures; Mary Marvel; Captain Marvel Jr.;* and *The Marvel Family. Captain Marvel Adventures* was the highest-selling comic book in the early 1940s, with some figures suggesting it sold 1.3 million copies a month in 1944. The sales success is usually attributed to the high quality of the stories and artwork, which were mostly written by Otto Binder, with C. C. Beck being the main artist on the line.

Harry Donenfeld was not pleased by the success of a comic that he felt infringed on his Superman character: both heroes were superstrong, superfast dark-haired muscular men who were invulnerable. He sent a cease and desist letter to Fawcett, who had received another such letter already from DC, concerning an earlier hero, Master Man. They had complied then, but now Fawcett Comics fought back and argued that Captain Marvel was different enough from Superman to be his own unique hero, specifically arguing that the whole "young boy magically transforms into a adult hero" idea was different enough from Superman to make the character unique, even if Captain Marvel himself appeared similar to Superman. Donenfeld responded by suing Fawcett for copyright infringement in 1941.

The case did not go to trial until 1948. DC was represented by the famed trial attorney Louis Nizer. In the first trial, while the judge determined that Captain Marvel did, in fact, infringe upon Superman's copyright, Fawcett's lawyers argued that due to the omission of a copyright notice on some early Superman strips DC had forfeited the copyright on Superman. The judge agreed and determined that DC had, indeed, abandoned the copyright on Superman.

DC appealed to the United States Court of Appeals for the Second Circuit, where the legendary judge Learned Hand ruled that DC's copyright was, in fact, valid. On the infringement issue, though, he issued a mixed ruling. He determined that Captain Marvel himself was not a copy of Superman, but the style of Captain Marvel's stories was an infringement of the Superman stories. By this time it was 1952, and sales of Fawcett's superhero comics had dropped dramatically, to the point where, in the early 1950s, they were already trying to use more of a horror style in the Captain Marvel line of titles. Fawcett determined that it just wasn't financially prudent to keep fighting DC, so it settled in 1952, paid DC $400,000, and ceased publication of its superhero comics.

A few decades later, DC approached Fawcett about using the Captain Marvel character itself, and Fawcett agreed to license the character. However, an interesting twist to the story occurred in the ensuing decades. During the 1960s, Marvel Comics became a major force in the comic industry, and Stan Lee was extremely creative when it came to picking up names that he found striking, taking, for instance, the name Daredevil, in 1964, from an out-of-business superhero comic of the 1940s. In 1967, perhaps inspired by a small company using the name themselves for a short-lived series in 1966, he created a new Captain Marvel character and quickly trademarked the name.

Therefore when DC licensed Captain Marvel from Fawcett, it could not call its comic *Captain Marvel* anymore, because Marvel Comics now had a trademark on that name. So the book's title was changed to *Shazam!*

Captain Marvel remained popular, even gaining his own television series in the 1970s (also called *Shazam!*). Eventually, DC purchased the rights

© DC Comics

to the Captain Marvel line of characters from Fawcett entirely. Due to the ensuing trademark situation, Marvel knows that it has to publish a comic with the name *Captain Marvel* on a fairly regular basis (at least once every few years), because if it ever lapses in publishing such a title, DC will certainly swoop in and try to get the trademark terminated. It puts Marvel in an interesting position, as the character Captain Marvel has never sold particularly well for it, but it will no doubt keep trying new versions of the character, mostly just to maintain the trademark.

EDITOR JULIUS SCHWARTZ was the brains behind the so-called Silver Age of comics (generally considered to be from the late 1950s until the very early 1970s), which began when he started introducing the first new superheroes at DC Comics since the 1940s, starting with the introduction of the new Flash in *Showcase* #4 in 1956. When revamping characters, he never forgot his creative roots, and in one case paid a particularly interesting homage.

As a teenager, Schwartz was a fan of science fiction, and in 1932 he started one of the very first fan magazines devoted to science fiction. A couple of years later, while still a teenager, Schwartz became a literary agent for science fiction writers, working with such legendary authors as Ray Bradbury and H. P. Lovecraft (the former at the beginning of his stellar career, the latter at the conclusion). During the 1940s, Schwartz got a job working as an assistant editor at All-American Comics, which would merge with DC Comics in 1944. While working at DC, Schwartz always tried to take care of the science fiction writers he knew, getting them work whenever he could.

Schwartz was tasked with creating new versions of some of DC's superheroes of the 1940s, and after the Flash debuted in 1956 in a comic anthology, Schwartz gave the writing assignment for the character's ongoing title to John Broome, a science fiction writer he had known as a teen. In 1959 Broome would relaunch another 1940s hero, with the creation of the new Green Lantern.

The next relaunch was of the Atom. The original Atom, Al Pratt, was one of the lesser lights of All-American Comics, as he was a short man (five foot one) who learned how to box and then threw on a mask and a cape and fought crime as a member of the Justice Society of America. Eventually, in 1948, probably concerned with his relative lack of powers, he was given super strength.

The new Atom, however, was a scientist who developed a belt made out of "white dwarf star matter," which allowed him to shrink to subatomic size. While at this size, he would be able to control his weight, so he could, for instance, while tiny hit someone with the force of his full weight behind him, which was an effective tool for knocking bad guys out. The name of the new

© Mary Evans Picture Library, courtesy of Pierre Tardif

Atom was Ray Palmer, which is the name of a science fiction editor friend of Julie Schwartz. The joke was that Raymond A. Palmer was an actual dwarf.

When he was seven years old, Palmer was hit by a truck, and an unsuccessful operation on his spine resulted in the stunting of his growth (he stood four feet tall) and the development of a hunchback. Palmer found a refuge from his physical problems in the pages of science fiction books, and he soon became a prolific writer himself and the editor of the prominent science fiction magazine *Amazing Stories* from 1938 to 1949. There he had the distinction of purchasing Isaac Asimov's first professional story. Palmer was well known for his sense of humor, so he certainly appreciated his friend's odd homage to him.

COMIC BOOK COMPANIES have never really done much in the way of market research. For most of the history of comics, there just was not the money in the budget for detailed research into why any title was selling or just what the sales figures for each book were. At DC Comics during the 1950s, deciding why books were selling was the job of the publisher, Irwin Donenfeld, and the methods he used were not exactly the most scientific.

At one point, early on in the fifties, Donenfeld asked Julie Schwartz about a particular issue of the science fiction comic Schwartz was editing, *Strange Adventures*. The sales for the issue were significantly higher than for previous issues. The two men brainstormed, and all they could come up with was that perhaps the cover, which featured a man trapped in the body of a gorilla in a jail cell, appealed to children. Perhaps they liked gorillas?

So they put a gorilla on the cover of another comic book, and the sales went up. They put a gorilla on another comic, and sales went up too. Soon Schwartz was putting gorillas on the covers of so many books that Donenfeld had to step in and make a rule—only one cover with a gorilla on it per month!

Similar reasoning determined a cover motif that frequently occurred on Schwartz's science fiction titles: every time the cover showed the earth in an odd position, like from a strange angle or being cut in half or anything of that sort, sales went up. As you can imagine, soon they were trying to put the earth into as many bizarre scenarios as they could come up with.

Later in the 1950s, the most popular image to feature on a comic cover was a *Tyrannosaurus rex* (although gorilla covers were still popular even then). Soon tyrannosaurs were everywhere. You knew things were getting out of hand when *Tomahawk*, DC's Western title about a government operative during the American Revolution, had tyrannosaurs on the covers of multiple issues!

It was bad enough when DC was making decisions based solely on how covers seemed to sell; it was quite another matter when Marvel Comics became a major sales force in the 1960s. DC had to examine both its sales and Marvel's sales, and see what Marvel was doing right that they were not.

The problem was that DC was so used to being the industry standard that it really could not comprehend how Marvel could possibly be passing it by. It did not make sense to them, and some of the ideas they came up with to combat Marvel's sales seem, in retrospect, quite bizarre.

The first theory DC developed was that Marvel was doing well because its comic book covers employed "bad art"; that is, art that was so unsophisticated that it appealed to children, who did not want to be challenged by artwork. This might not have been something Donenfeld came up with, but whoever made the determination forced at least one DC title, *Wonder Woman*, to specifically change its art style to be less detailed and less professional. Since the title went back to its original style within a year, it is unlikely that the change was an effective one.

The next theory was a bit more informed and was based on the way comics were displayed on store magazine racks or on spinner racks. On a magazine rack, comics would be placed in tiers, with the latest books going on the first tier, and the older books going behind

© DC Comics

them. The new books would block all but the top of the older books. Likewise, in a spinner rack often all that would be recognizable would be the tops of the books. Donenfeld felt that the best way to use this to DC's advantage was to make sure the tops of their books looked unique, so he added black-and-white checkered boxes to the tops of all DC comics.

Apparently, sales went up during the time of the "go-go checks" (as they were called by staffers), but this was just before DC was purchased by

Warner Bros. When it was, Donenfeld was out as publisher, and once he departed, the new publisher eliminated the checkered boxes from the covers.

BY 1963 DC had been publishing *Justice League of America* (a remake of *Justice Society of America*), for a number of years. Although it featured a number of its superheroes in one book, the various characters of the DC Universe had kept mostly to themselves. In fact, the editors of *Superman* and *Batman* each insisted that their heroes involvement in the Justice League be downplayed (this was the same during the 1940s, when both Superman and Batman were technically members of the Justice Society of America, though they rarely appeared). So when it was published in 1963, *The Brave and the Bold* #50 was, for the time, significant: that was when the title turned into a team-up book, pairing DC heroes, some of whom had never appeared with each other in a comic book story.

In the fifth issue using this format, *The Brave and the Bold* #54, three teen sidekicks of DC heroes meet one another. Batman's sidekick Robin, the Flash's sidekick Kid Flash, and Aquaman's sidekick Aqualad all team up to defeat a villain. Six issues later, the group was back, this time calling themselves the Teen Titans, and with a new member, Wonder Girl, presumably Wonder Woman's sidekick.

The question most readers of DC comics asked at the time was, "Who is Wonder Girl?" and it is a question that came about because the writer of the story, Bob Haney, accidentally used a character that did not yet exist.

As mentioned earlier, the DC titles were generally run like little

© DC Comics

kingdoms, where the characters were guarded, even from other creators. Therefore, there was no communication between Haney and the writer-editor of *Wonder Woman*, Robert Kanigher. If there had been communication, Haney would have learned who the Wonder Girl character actually was. Kanigher had done a few flashback stories with Wonder Woman as a child in the late 1950s, and they proved popular. He then did some stories with Wonder Woman as a young toddler, and they too were popular. So Kanigher came up with a rather odd idea, although another popular one, which was that Wonder Woman would team up with herself as a child and as a toddler! Kanigher wrote a number of issues (they were called "impossible stories") where the three characters would team up, along with Wonder Woman's mother, Queen Hippolyta.

When Haney was putting together his team of teen heroes, he saw one of Kanigher's issues and presumed that the girl was Wonder Woman's sidekick, not a younger version of Wonder Woman herself. So he added her to the Teen Titans.

Eventually given her own name, Donna Troy, Wonder Girl would serve as a member of the Teen Titans for years, and over the years many different writers have attempted to explain away Haney's original mistake, usually just succeeding in making her origins more confusing. It is probably hard to come up with a good origin for a character when her real origin was essentially an "oops."

THE TEEN TITANS were given their own series in 1966, but the book soon began to flounder a bit from lack of direction. Toward the end of the decade, while they were trying to break into the comic book industry, Marv Wolfman and Len Wein were given a chance at writing the title. The pair was barely out of their teens at the time (Wolfman was twenty-three, Wein twenty-one). As they were attempting to distinguish themselves, they tried to do something that was yet to be done at DC Comics—introduce an African American superhero.

Marvel, which was the far looser and more liberal company, only had a handful of African American heroes itself at the time. At the conservative DC Comics of the 1960s, it would be an extremely big deal. The story was written by Wolfman and Wein, and drawn by the book's regular artist, Nick Cardy. It was about a hooded hero named Jericho, who tries to keep a group of African American gang members from being incited to violence by the mob. Eventually the hood comes off, and he is revealed to be the brother of a member of the gang.

Right before the book was to go to print, the new publisher of DC, Carmine Infantino, pulled the book. Infantino never went into specifics, saying only that he would not let the book go out as written. Neal Adams, a star artist at DC at the time, attempted to step in and quell the anger that Wolfman and Wein were feeling over their story being rejected, and in the end Adams ended up reworking and redrawing most of the issue in the span of a weekend so the book would be ready to go to press. The new story involved a Caucasian hero named Joshua and gang members that were not race specific. Outrage over the incident resulted in Wolfman and Wein being blacklisted at DC for a number of years.

Eventually, both men returned to work for DC, and in the 1980s Wolfman had some measure of revenge. He was writing the follow-up book to the *Teen Titans*, the *New Teen Titans*, and it was DC's highest-selling book at the time. A few years into his run, he introduced a new member of the Titans. His name? Jericho. Granted, this new Jericho was also a Caucasian, but still, fifteen years later Wolfman got to use the name.

* * *

MARV WOLFMAN WAS also involved in another interesting incident at DC in the late 1960s; this time it involved the Comics Code Authority, specifically a loophole for getting around it.

The Comics Code Authority was the result of the public-relations disaster the comic book industry suffered when the psychiatrist Fredric Wertham began a campaign against what he felt was, as he titled his book on the subject, the *Seduction of the Innocent*. (See page 42 for Wertham's previous effects on DC's comics.) Ultimately, Wertham caused a big enough stir that Senator Estes Kefauver, the same man who went after organized crime in the 1950s, decided to have a congressional hearing investigating Wertham's claims against comic books. Ultimately too frightened about the notion of the government regulating comics, the Comics Magazine Association of America decided to police itself, forming the Comics Code Authority, a committee that rated comic books and judged whether they were appropriate for children. In the 1950s, you needed to have the "Comics Code Approved" seal if you wanted stores to sell your comics.

The initial Comics Code regulations were themselves practically obscene in what they disallowed. The strict rules demanded that stories were prohibited from including anything that would show disrespect for authority. Drugs were out, even if they were shown to be evil. Also, stories had to end with good triumphing over evil—no matter what. The words *crime, horror,* and *terror* were all banned from comic book titles (something that EC Comics' owner Charles Gaines felt was specifically meant to hurt his comics line, which included titles with each of those words). Most amusingly, vampires, werewolves, ghouls, and zombies were all banned from comics, because everyone knows that the number one cause of juvenile delinquency is vampires. It is this last restriction that is at issue here.

In 1969 Wolfman was contributing stories to DC's horror

anthology *House of Secrets* (one can only imagine what you had to do for horror stories when you could not use vampires, werewolves, etc.). As noted above, you could not even mention werewolves or wolfmen by name inside the comic. However, a spark of an idea hit Gerry Conway, the editor of the comic. He asked, "Even if that is the fellow's name?" In that case, they said, it *would* be allowed.

The result was *House of Secrets* #83. During that period, each of the various horror anthologies was "hosted" by a character. Cain was the host of the *House of Mystery*, and his brother Abel was the host of the *House of Secrets*. So before one of the stories, Abel tells the reader that the following story was told to him by a "wandering wolfman," and on the very next page is: "Script: Marv Wolfman."

An amusing side effect of Conway's attempt to mock the Comics Code Authority was that the other writers of the book were a bit displeased. At the time, there were no credits in the DC horror anthologies. So once Wolfman was given one, everyone wanted one, and soon the books were filled with the names of all the creative staff for the issue.

WHILE THE TEEN Titans gained their own comic book series in 1966, DC Comics gained its own teen titan that same year when it hired Jim Shooter. He was only fourteen years old!

Shooter was an avid comic book reader, and while recuperating from an illness, he was reading a load of comics and noting to himself that the comics from DC seemed to lack the excitement of the Marvel comics of the same period. So Shooter, at the tender age of fourteen, decided to pick the book he felt could most use his skills (ego was never much of a problem during Shooter's career) and decided *Adventure Comics*, which had a Legion of Super-Heroes feature, would be the one. He wrote and drew a proposed script and sent it to editor Mort Weisinger. Weisinger liked the script a lot, and upon contacting Shooter was stunned to find that he was only fourteen.

Luckily for Shooter, Weisinger was more receptive to children than most people in his position would be. Weisinger was known for surveying children to see what they were interested in, then putting them into the stories of the comics he edited. He would even purchase cover ideas from children, under the theory that if one twelve-year-old thinks it is a great idea, it is likely that other twelve-year-olds would agree. He purchased a cover idea from Cary Bates when he was twelve, and later hired him to write when he was only seventeen years old. So if a kid was going to pitch to anyone, Weisinger would be the one. He hired Shooter, and after some changes were made, the script Shooter sent in was published in

Adventure Comics #346. Shooter would go on to write the Legion feature until he retired from comics, a grizzled veteran at eighteen.

However, he would return to comics in the mid-1970s, and by the end of the decade he was editor in chief of Marvel Comics, a position he held for a number of years. Shooter would go on to create three new comic book companies over the years: Valiant (which was purchased by Acclaim Entertainment for sixty-five million dollars in 1994), Defiant, and Broadway.

In 2008 the fifty-six-year-old Shooter returned to the Legion as the regular writer of DC's *Legion of Superheroes*.

WHILE CLEARLY NONE of his other creations will ever be as popular or as influential as Superman, Jerry Siegel helped created a number of other lasting characters, with and without Joe Shuster. One of the Shuster-less creations was the Spectre, who made his debut in 1940, in *More Fun Comics* #58. The story behind the Spectre is that hard-nosed cop Jim Corrigan is murdered, but finds his way to Heaven barred. He has to stay on Earth as the ghostly Spectre, meting out vengeance on the evil and armed with powerful magic abilities that allow him to come up with creative ways to hurt the bad guys.

The stories with the Spectre were fairly gruesome by the standards of comics in the 1940s. He had strange and cruel ways of punishing evildoers, starting with the men who murdered Corrigan. The Spectre was a popular character throughout the early part of the 1940s, but by the middle of the decade his popularity had waned, and for a time, he was forced to play guardian angel for a bumbling character called Percival Popp. Then, just before World War II ended in 1945, Jim Corrigan somehow enlisted in the army, and the Spectre disappeared for decades.

The Spectre was one of a few 1940s characters brought back in the 1960s, after the success of the early reboots like the Flash and Green Lantern. He received his own title again in 1967, but it was short-lived. He would not return again until an editor at DC Comics had an unfortunate encounter on a New York City street.

Joe Orlando was editing the comic anthology *Adventure Comics*, and he was debating what new character should take over the lead feature. During this time, he was mugged on the streets in New York. Orlando was furious over what had happened to him, and with his fury came a desire to seek some sort of vengeance upon the crooks, which led directly to Michael Fleisher's Spectre series in *Adventure Comics*.

Fleisher, along with artist Jim Aparo, began a series with the Spectre as the lead feature in *Adventure Comics* #431. The run was not long (ending with #440), but it was memorable, with Fleisher's Spectre coming up with increasingly sadistic ways of killing off criminals, like turning them into wood then putting them through a jigsaw, or turning them into glass and smashing them, or turning them into wax and melting them. Whatever their death was, it was always poetic. Orlando must have been delighted to live vicariously through the painful revenge the Spectre delivered to the crooks.

The series would have a strange postscript, which came about in a comics magazine, the *Comics Journal*. While being interviewed in 1979, author Harlan Ellison began discussing Fleisher's Spectre and remarked that to write stories like that Fleisher must be, among other terms (some crasser), "crazy," "certifiable," a "lunatic." Fleisher then sued Ellison and the *Comics Journal* for libel, ultimately losing in 1986.

ALMOST TEN YEARS after Wolfman and Wein's *Teen Titans* story was pulled (see pages 65–66), DC still had yet to give an African American superhero his or her own series. DC decided to finally address this by creating a title featuring an African American hero, but the first attempt ended with an extremely bizarre (and fairly offensive) concept that luckily never saw print.

Writer Tony Isabella, who had written a number of issues for two African American superheroes over at Marvel, Power Man and Black

Goliath, was approached by DC to take over a new series it had not yet debuted. Scripts were in for the first two issues, and the title was to be called *The Black Bomber*. It would star a Caucasian Vietnam veteran who, due to the side effects of some experiments he underwent while in Vietnam (to better camouflage troops), turns into an African American man at night and fights crime as the Black Bomber. When he was his normal identity, though, he was a bigot, à la Archie Bunker on *All in the Family*.

Isabella luckily convinced DC not to publish the title but rather to let him create a new character. The end result was Black Lightning, who was Jefferson Pierce, a former Olympic decathlete who comes back to his old neighborhood to teach, and finds the neighborhood being run by the 100, a local criminal group. Pierce and a friend devise a costume, along with a belt that would allow him to fire electricity, and he begins to fight crime as Black Lightning.

Black Lightning has been one of the more popular African American heroes in comics, although he has been unable to sustain his own title for any long period of time. He is currently a member of the Justice League of America.

Unlike most other creators, Isabella was able to work out a creator-incentive plan with DC for the creation of Black Lightning, resulting in a certain amount of profit sharing for Isabella. One area where he was specifically compensated was for any use of Black Lightning in other media. He would be paid a royalty for use in television or film.

During the 1970s, DC's superhero characters were licensed to Hanna-Barbera to use in the popular animated series *Super Friends*. In the late 1970s, Hanna-Barbera expanded the cast of the show and changed its name to *The Challenge of the Super Friends*. Hanna-Barbera wanted to use Black Lightning, but DC informed them that if they used Black Lightning, they would have to pay a higher licensing fee to cover Isabella's separate royalty fee. Rather than pay him the fee, Hanna-Barbera just created their own analogue for Black Lightning called Black Vulcan.

Black Vulcan also had lightning powers; the only notable difference (besides his pantless costume) was that he could fly. Understandably,

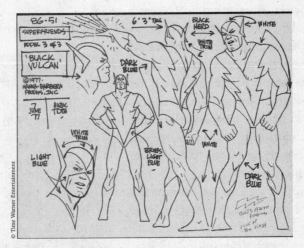

Alex Toth's design sheet for Black Vulcan's appearance in *Super Friends*, from the personal collection of Ruben Espinosa.

Isabella was displeased about this situation, so in an issue of *Black Lightning* he had a con artist name Barbara Hanna show up along with an impostor Black Lightning. To this date, Black Lightning has yet to appear on any DC Comics–licensed television series.

© DC Comics

SPEAKING OF ANALOGOUS characters, does the following character sound familiar? A young boy with dark hair, who wears glasses and has a forehead scar. The boy is a powerful magician. The boy has a pet owl. Everyone knows who this is, right? It has to be . . . Tim Hunter?

Tim Hunter was created by Neil Gaiman in DC's *Books of Magic* #1, published in 1990. The series follows the young boy as he is met by magical characters from other DC Comics titles, who take him on a journey through the history of magic in the DC Universe, while preparing Hunter for the fact that he might grow up to be the most powerful magician in the world.

J. K. Rowling's popular Harry Potter book series did not start until seven years later, in 1997. In fact, Rowling has even gone on record as saying that she came up with the idea in the same year that *Books of Magic* was released (both Gaiman and Rowling are British writers).

However, while the works may appear similar, it is highly unlikely that

© Thomas Taylor, Warner Brothers

it is anything more than an amusing coincidence. A writer who backs up that position is none other than the possible "wronged" party in this instance, writer Neil Gaiman. He has detailed on more than one occasion the fact that he does not believe that Rowling was influenced by his work, but rather that both he and she were drawing from the same cultural influences, specifically T. H. White's work (particularly *The Sword in the Stone*, about a young boy who is destined to be King Arthur—also with a pet owl).

ONE COMPANY THAT was less than thrilled with the similarities it found between its intellectual property and a comic book character was Charles Atlas Ltd., which got involved in a trademark-infringement case via one of the odder routes one could imagine.

In 1989 Grant Morrison began writing the DC series *Doom Patrol* with issue #19. The book was not doing very well at the time, so the young British writer was given free rein to try whatever he could to resurrect it, much in the same way that, five years earlier, Morrison's fellow Brit Alan Moore was given free rein with *Swamp Thing*. That title had become one of the most critically acclaimed books of the decade. Morrison's take on the Doom Patrol, a team of out-the-ordinary superheroes, was to make them truly out of the ordinary, adding to the team a woman with multiple personalities (each one having a separate superpower), a little girl with a face like an ape who had powerful "imaginary friends," and a living street.

© DC Comics

The book became even weirder as Morrison got more comfortable in his run, but the results were increased sales and critical acclaim. In 1990, in *Doom Patrol* #35, the team encountered Flex

Mentallo, who was a parody of the famous bodybuilder Charles Atlas. Essentially, Mentallo was what became of the "wimp getting sand kicked in his face at the beach" from the famous Charles Atlas ads.

The character proved so popular that even after he left the title, Morrison wrote a critically acclaimed 1996 miniseries starring Flex Mentallo, in which the reader discovers that superheroes exist, but they are hiding in our imaginations, in fear of a being called the Absolute. All four issues of the series examine the very notion of what it means to create something. It is a brilliant work, so good that a fan of the series thought that the people at Charles Atlas would be thrilled to hear that their founder was involved in such a brilliant work. Well, they were not thrilled.

Charles Atlas Ltd. sued DC Comics for trademark infringement. Although DC was ultimately granted a motion for summary judgment using a "parody" defense, since the trial DC has refused to reprint the series. Morrison has also made amends with the fan, who certainly did not mean to cause such a problem.

BEING A SUBSIDIARY of a large corporation has made DC Comics a bit conservative at times when it comes to the content it provides. At the same time, DC Comics' Vertigo imprint of "mature readers only" titles, including the aforementioned *Doom Patrol*, *Swamp Thing*, and *Books of Magic*, is one of the most diverse lines of sophisticated comic book stories produced by a mainstream publisher—so they are not complete sticks in the mud. Still (as already noted on page 31), DC is familiar with pulping comic books for various interesting reasons. Here are three of their more notable pulled comics.

As noted a couple of times already, Alan Moore's *Swamp Thing* was an acclaimed comic book series in the 1980s. The title began as a standard horror comic book in 1972, but an incredibly well-crafted horror comic, with strong stories from writer Len Wein and dark, moody artwork by Bernie Wrightson. The book was popular enough to merit a film adaptation in the early 1980s (directed by Wes Craven). Based on the release of the film, the Swamp Thing was given his own series again. The original story was that a scientist, Alec

Holland, was working in a lab in the middle of a swamp when he was caught in a chemical explosion that transformed him into a, well, swamp thing, a humanoid made up of vegetable matter.

When Moore took over the title, he revealed that Holland had died in the explosion, and the chemicals had animated a group of vegetation into thinking it was Holland. After this bizarre turn of events, Moore used the title to explore a number of ecological and spiritual matters, while also using Swamp Thing to explore the darker side of the DC Universe. When Moore left the book, he was replaced by the man who was drawing the comic at the time, Rick Veitch.

Veitch continued in the same vein as Moore, although his most notable story line had Swamp Thing travel through time, meeting the various DC characters from different time periods (DC had books set in prehistoric times, Revolutionary War times, etc.). However, at one point toward the end of the story line (and soon before Veitch was set to leave the book on his own accord), Veitch had Swamp Thing encounter Jesus Christ.

The story had been approved by editorial and was already drawn, but, perhaps with an eye toward the current scandal surrounding Martin Scorsese's *The Last Temptation of Christ*, DC refused to release the issue. Veitch quit the book, and Neil Gaiman, who was set to follow Veitch's run along with writer Jamie Delano, refused to take over the book on principle.

THE STORY OF how Alan Moore returned to work for DC Comics at the turn of the twenty-first century is an interesting one in and of itself. After some disputes with DC over various issues (including putting parental warnings on its comics, refusal to pay Moore certain royalties he felt were owed him, and his general irritation that DC planned on keeping his works in print indefinitely, thereby preventing him from ever recovering the rights to them), Moore refused to ever work for them again. It is with that in mind that he signed a deal with comic book creator Jim Lee's company, Wildstorm, to pro-

duce a line of comics called America's Best Comics. Soon after the deal was signed (and with the books already in production), Lee sold his company to none other than DC Comics.

After promising that there would be a "firewall" of sorts between

Moore and DC, Moore agreed to continue to work for America's Best Comics. However, the firewall did not hold up for long: DC destroyed an entire issue of a Moore title in 2000 in order to make a change in the book.

Years earlier, Moore had a dispute with Marvel Comics over work he had done for its United Kingdom branch. Marvel had reprinted some of his work without his permission, and in retaliation he has denied permission to reprint the work since then. He made one short-lived exception in 2002, after some entreaties from Marvel, where he let them put out a volume of his work on their Captain Britain character. Marvel proceeded to leave his credit off of the collection (by mistake, presumably), leading to Moore once again cutting ties with the company. In any event, during the year 2000 there was still bad blood between Moore and Marvel. That was what was in DC's mind when it saw an ad in the back of its *League of Extraordinary Gentlemen* #5.

League of Extraordinary Gentlemen was a book set in England in the late 1890s, starring notable literary characters that had gone into the public domain, such as Dr. Jekyll/Mr. Hyde and Captain Nemo. The book was designed by artist Kevin O'Neill as though it was actually published in the late 1890s, and the back of the issue included historically accurate ads from Victorian newspapers. In #5, O'Neill placed in the back of the issue an actual ad, from an English newspaper of the era, for a female sanitary product with the brand name Marvel.

Fearing a reprisal from Marvel, DC had the entire issue's print run pulped and reprinted sans ad.

IN 2001 DC struck again, this time with a different America's Best Comic, Moore's anthology title, *Tomorrow Stories*, which collected different stories written by Moore and drawn by various artists. This time the tale in question was in *Tomorrow Stories* #8, and it dealt with Scientology.

The Church of Scientology has always been fairly quick to litigate to protect its reputation, so DC was concerned that it would be hit with a lawsuit if it included a short story in *Tomorrow Stories* #8 that involved two characters discussing a story about Scientology founder L. Ron Hubbard and an event he supposedly took part in with occultist John Whiteside Parsons. The issue had not gone to print yet, so DC removed the story. As a result, Moore, who had begun to slowly mend his bridges with DC and even approved a special commemorative edition of his classic series *Watchmen*, pulled back from DC once more. The story later appeared in an anthology by Top Shelf Productions (which currently produces the majority of Moore's new comic work, since he finally cut all ties with DC Comics in 2008).

The strangest thing about the situation, which resulted in DC ostracizing Moore, was that DC Comics had already published the same story Moore had the characters discuss! In 1995 DC's Paradox Press line of books had recounted the same story about Hubbard and Parsons in *The Big Book of Conspiracies*, and there was no lawsuit from the Church of Scientology.

Part Two

MARVEL COMICS

Timely Comics was one of the many comic book publishers that sprung up in the wake of the success of *Superman* at National Comics. Martin Goodman, like Harry Donenfeld, was a pulp magazine publisher before getting into the comic business. In the very first comic published by Timely, *Marvel Comics* #1, Goodman used stories he purchased from outside comic "packagers," who created prepackaged comic book stories to sell to the multitude of new publishers making superhero comics. Soon, though, Timely began producing its own stories, including its biggest success, Joe Simon (the top editor at Timely) and Jack Kirby's *Captain America*, which became one of the biggest-selling comics in the business. After Simon and Kirby left Timely, a young relative of Goodman's took over as the head writer-editor. His name was Stanley Lieber, but he wrote under the pseudonym Stan Lee.

After the war, superheroes went belly-up, so during the 1950s Timely (now calling itself Atlas Comics) would follow whatever trend was popular at a given time. Westerns, romance, young adult stories, science fiction—whatever was selling in the industry, Atlas produced. Finally, at the beginning of the 1960s, inspired by DC Comics' return to superheroes, Marvel (another name change) began introducing its own superheroes. Stan Lee and Jack Kirby spent the 1960s creating some of the most popular characters of the century, such as the Fantastic Four, the X-Men, the Hulk, and Spider-Man (Spider-Man was created by Lee with a different artist, Steve Ditko). By the early 1970s, Marvel Comics' line of superheroes was outselling DC's, most likely the first time since superheroes were introduced that DC was not the number one highest-selling comic book company.

Marvel has been the highest-selling comic company ever since (with occasional surges by DC pushing Marvel temporarily to number two). After being purchased by Ronald Perelman in the late 1980s, Marvel Comics went public in 1991, then went bankrupt in 1996, but eventually Marvel's subsidiary Toy Biz (now Marvel Toys) took control of the company and brought Marvel back into the black, mostly through money earned by turning Marvel properties into films. Recently, Marvel set up its own movie studio and has started producing its own films, starting with *Iron Man* in 2008 and planned films starring Thor, Captain America, and other Marvel heroes.

4

THE FANTASTIC FOUR

The *Fantastic Four* was the fruit of one of the longest-lasting and most successful collaborations in comic book history. Stan Lee and Jack Kirby produced the first 102 issues of the series together, from the book's debut in 1961 until Kirby left Marvel for DC in 1970.

The Fantastic Four is the story of Reed Richards, a scientist who insists on testing a spaceship he built (in the original comics it was built to "beat the Commies to the moon"; later stories changed that to "the stars" and downplayed the whole "Commie" angle). Reed sneaks into the ship with his girlfriend, his best friend, and his girlfriend's kid brother. While in outer space, the ship is bombarded by cosmic rays, and when the ship comes back to Earth, each of the four has gained fantastic powers. Reed can stretch his body like it is rubber; his girlfriend, Sue, can turn invisible; her brother, Johnny, can turn into living flame; and Reed's best friend, Ben, has become a monstrous rocklike thing of a man. They agree to use their new powers to help mankind.

The book was notable for two reasons. First, because the Fantastic Four was the first superhero team that was more like a family than other groups, partly because Sue (the Invisible Girl/Woman) and Johnny (the Human Torch) are brother and sister, but even more so because the four of them interact very much in the way families interact (including bickering). Second, the tragedy of Ben Grimm, who takes the name the Thing, gives the book a strong emotional core. Reed (Mr. Fantastic) is constantly searching for a cure for his friend's condition, while Ben comes to terms with the fact that while he looks like a monster he is still a man.

Early in the book's run, they encounter an old college rival of Reed's who becomes the group's most notable enemy, Doctor Doom. For the rest of their run, Lee and Kirby would constantly introduce new characters into the series, the most notable being the world-devouring Galactus and his herald, the Silver Surfer, who searches for worlds for Galactus to feed on until kindness from an earthling causes him to rebel against his master.

The Fantastic Four have starred in numerous animated televisions series based on the comic, and recently they were featured in two successful motion pictures (a third film in the series may be forthcoming).

THE GENESIS OF the Fantastic Four is one of the most widely told tales in the comic book industry. As the legend goes, Martin Goodman was out golfing with the publisher of DC Comics, Irwin Donenfeld (some versions have it as DC chief Jack Liebowitz instead), and while they were golfing, Donenfeld remarked that DC was having quite a success with its new superhero-team book, *Justice League of America*. As soon as they were done golfing, Goodman got on the phone to Stan Lee and told him that Marvel needed to create a new superhero-team book.

© DC Comics

The dates certainly work, as the Justice League had made its debut in the pages of *The Brave and the Bold* #28 in early 1960 before quickly graduating to its own book later that same year.

However, both Donenfeld and Liebowitz denied ever playing golf with Goodman, let alone playing golf and bragging about the sales of *Justice League of America*. Film producer Michael Uslan has put forth the alternate theory—courtesy of DC's production manager at the time, Sol Harrison—that it was actually someone from Independent News, the distributor for both Marvel and DC's comics at the time, who told Goodman. Independent News would have had the sales figures for both companies, and Paul Sampliner, the head of Independent News, did know Goodman. That theory makes a good deal more sense.

Whether the Sampliner version is true or not, the end of the story is accurate, which is that Goodman discovered that DC was doing good numbers with a superhero-team book, so he notified Lee and said that Marvel had to produce a superhero-team book as well. Lee produced the comic, but before he did so, he was already considering a move that would have dramatically changed comic book history.

MARVEL COMICS (or Atlas Comics, as it was called at the time) suffered through a very difficult decade in the 1950s. Sales of the books had dipped very low, and costs were being cut all over the company. Artists were going from being paid forty dollars per page to twenty-five dollars per page. John Romita, who later became one of the more famous Marvel superhero artists, recalls being fired by Stan Lee via Lee's secretary.

Eventually, Marvel's eight titles were, more or less, being written and edited by one man, Lee, and drawn by three or four artists—Jack Kirby, Steve Ditko, and Joe Maneely being the most prodigious. These artists, while talented, were kept around mostly because they could produce work quickly—they would be able to draw an entire line of comics in a month. These working conditions are what led to what is now known as the "Marvel method" of writing a comic book. Since he was writing so many titles, Lee did not have the time to write out full scripts for each book. Instead, he would come up with rough plots that he would give to the artists to draw however they felt was best. Lee would then script the art they gave back to him.

Understandably, this work was not the most gratifying for Lee. Writing eight low-selling comic books a month and overseeing a company that was in the pits was not where Lee saw himself. He chose to write comics under the pseudonym Stan Lee because he had planned on reserving his given name for "real" writing.

So when Martin Goodman told Lee that he wanted him to come up with a team of superheroes to match DC's Justice League, Lee's instinct was to quit comics altogether. He was thirty-nine years old at the time and felt he was too old to be going back to the type of stories he had told when he was literally a teenager. His wife ultimately talked him out of it by suggesting that, instead of quitting, he should just tell the type of stories he wanted to tell, and if it ended up failing, then he would be no worse off than if he had quit. Lee agreed to stay and went out of his way to create characters he himself would be interested in reading, and the result was one of most successful comic book series of all time (of course, it did not hurt to have a comic book legend like Jack Kirby creating the comic with him).

PERHAPS ONE OF the most controversial aspects of Marvel Comics' great success in the 1960s is how much of the credit to attribute to the various creators involved in the production of the comics. A good deal of the behind-the-scenes workings were not publicized, and when readers hear about them now, they often get a false impression of how the process worked. In the ensuing discussions,

Stan Lee often gets a bit of a short shrift, particularly from fans who believe that Jack Kirby was the sole writer of the later issues of *The Fantastic Four*.

As noted earlier, since Lee wrote a great deal of the comics using the so-called Marvel method, that is how Lee and Kirby initially worked together on *The Fantastic Four*. In fact, at first the two would have long discussions over the plots of the issues, with both of them determining the general plot outline, which Kirby would then draw, and Lee script.

However, as Marvel Comics became more popular, the workload for Lee increased, particularly in the fields outside of the writing arena. He had to take care of more editorial functions of the job. So the long plot discussions he once had with Kirby more or less vanished. Lee trusted that Kirby would come up with good plots on his own, and Lee would script those plots. The confusing part of this process to fans is that Kirby would include margin notes with his artwork. It would appear, from a glance, that Kirby was not only producing the plots but also giving Lee the dialogue, thus turning Lee into a glorified transcriber.

That was not the case. Kirby's margin notes were generally meant more as a mood indicator, telling Lee how Kirby meant a particular scene to play out emotionally. Was a scene meant to be funny, dramatic, sad—these sample dialogue notes by Kirby would get the point across to Lee when it came time to come up with the actual dialogue.

Even with these notes, though, Lee would routinely scrap Kirby's plans and do whatever he felt made for a better story. This grated on Kirby—he and Lee had diametrically opposed views concerning what it was that Kirby was delivering to Lee. Lee felt that he was being given a plot; Kirby felt that he was delivering a story and that Lee should not be changing it as he saw fit, which is exactly what Lee was doing. Lee would get his pages from Kirby, and then use the script he wrote to make changes, and since those changes would go into print, Kirby had to adapt the story in the next issue to accommodate them, because the changed versions were what the public was reading.

So for most of their run together, they could be termed coplotters, and Kirby the sole plotter for the later issues. There is one famous idea, though, that was completely Kirby's idea, and that was the Silver Surfer. Lee and Kirby came up with the idea of the world-devouring being Galactus, but there was no mention of Silver Surfer in that original plot. When he began drawings the pages, though, Kirby felt that someone as powerful as Galactus would have a herald, so he came up with the idea of the Silver Surfer flying ahead of Galactus to scope out worlds to eat. Lee loved the idea, and a star character was born.

WHEN *THE FANTASTIC Four* first came out, there was some concern at Marvel about whether DC would object to Marvel suddenly publishing superhero comics of its own (see pages 160–61 for why Marvel would care whether DC approved of what it published), and at the same time there was most likely some concern about whether superhero comics would sell at all for Marvel, which was doing really three types of stories at the time—Westerns, romances, and monster comics.

Whatever the precise reason for concern, the end result was an interesting approach to the covers of the first two issues of the *Fantastic Four*: Stan Lee very deliberately had Jack Kirby hide the fact that the *Fantastic Four* was a superhero comic. The covers of

the first two issues are practically indistinguishable from the Marvel monster books of the time. Most notably, none of the characters wears a costume and both covers prominently feature monsters.

© Marvel Comics, image courtesy of Greg Theakston

The original version of the cover for the third issue of *The Fantastic Four* followed in this vein.

It originally spotlighted the monster the group was fighting, but for whatever reason (perhaps sales determined that superheroes were workable, or perhaps after two issues and no complaints from DC, Marvel felt safe), the original cover was scrapped and a

© Marvel Comics

brand-new cover was created, proudly presenting the Fantastic Four as superheroes, complete with their matching costumes.

Interestingly enough, there was also a notable change made to the Fantastic Four's planned costumes. One of the notable aspects of the Four is that they are a rare group of superheroes whose identities are publicly known—they were the first celebrity superheroes. However, in the original version of *Fantastic Four* #3, where the group's costumes debut, their costumes all have masks. Even the monstrous-looking Thing has a goalielike mask! Luckily, someone thought twice, and the masks were scrapped before the issue went to press.

THE FANTASTIC FOUR made many enemies over the years, but rarely did they take on an adversary with as much bite as when they ran afoul of the Nixon administration in the mid-1970s.

As noted earlier (on page 39), comic companies tried to do everything they could to avoid raising prices. They would reduce the size of the comics, they would cut the page count, but what they tried not to do was to raise the price of comics, and indeed it stayed at ten cents for well over two decades. Finally in the early 1960s, the price of comics went to twelve cents. By the early 1970s, comics were fifteen cents at both Marvel and DC, but that's when a bit of a controversy stirred up.

Inflation was considered out of control in the early 1970s. The inflation rate in 1970 was 6 percent, and in the middle of 1971 it was 4 percent. Historically, those were abnormally high rates, and to deal with the out-of-control inflation President Richard Nixon instituted a wage-and-price-control policy in August of 1971. For ninety days, there would be a complete price freeze.

Soon before the policy was put into place, Marvel raised the price of its entire line of comics from fifteen cents to twenty-five cents (DC did the same around the same time). The next month, Marvel lowered the price back to twenty cents.

So there shouldn't be a problem, right? A price freeze would only affect *raising* prices, so Marvel would appear to be in the clear. However, when Marvel went from fifteen cents to twenty-five cents, it also increased the page count of the comics to make up for the price increase, but inflation had driven the costs of production up so much that Marvel could not afford to produce the extra pages, even at the higher price points. So it was now twenty cents for the same page count as their fifteen cent comics. Sneakily, Marvel had slipped in a percentage-price increase.

This did not slip past the Nixon administration, and after some back and forth, it determined a punishment for Marvel: in *Fantastic Four* #128, released in 1972, Marvel would include a free four-page insert in the middle of the comic, made out of glossy paper. That would serve as Marvel's way of giving back to its fans.

An interesting side note regarding the price changes is that this is where Marvel really benefited by being a smaller company. Since it was smaller, it was able to change prices extremely quickly. DC, as part of a large corporation, was much slower in moving, so it was stuck at the higher price point for almost a full year, causing it to compete with Marvel during that whole time while charging five cents more per book. It is likely not a coincidence, then, that early 1972 is when Marvel officially passed DC in total sales.

THE FANTASTIC FOUR have appeared on television in a variety of animated forms, but probably the strangest take on the concept was the 1978 animated series, produced by DePatie-Freleng Enterprises for the NBC television network. The series starred Mr. Fantastic, the Thing, Invisible Girl, and H.E.R.B.I.E. the robot?! Yes, this series did not feature the Human Torch, but instead placed a robot as the fourth member of the team (the robot was cocreated by Stan Lee and Jack Kirby, at least—the last time the two men worked together on a project). H.E.R.B.I.E. stood for Humanoid Experimental Robot, B-Type, Integrated Electronics.

Most viewers guessed that the reason for the exclusion of the Human Torch was that the producers of the show feared children

might attempt to emulate him by lighting themselves on fire. And in the 1980s, in an issue of *The Fantastic Four*, writer John Byrne had a child do just that, as an homage to the rumors (it also made for a powerful issue, starring Johnny, as he deals with his guilt over the incident). A producer who had worked on a Fantastic Four cartoon series even cited this as the reason why the Human Torch was not used (which was odd because, while he was a producer for a Fantastic Four cartoon, he was not the producer for this Fantastic Four cartoon, and on his cartoon the Human Torch did appear).

The truth was much simpler. After the success of *The Incredible Hulk*, Marvel licensed out a number of other heroes to Universal Studios for possible television series or made-for-television movies. One of these heroes was the Human Torch. The project went as far as to have a script written, but nothing was ever filmed (most likely due to the extreme difficulties of depicting a man on fire in the 1970s—it is difficult today, even with the aid of computer graphic effects, so it was incredibly difficult back then). Universal was not involved in the cartoon, and it would not make a deal to allow the Torch to be used, so he was omitted from the series.

As an interesting side note to the whole affair, a few years after the cartoon ended, the California studio where DePatie-Freleng Enterprises produced its shows was destroyed. How was it destroyed? The building burned to the ground.

ONE AMUSING THING about pop culture is that it often outlives the references it makes. One such example is the Fantastic Four's the Thing, who Stan Lee made purposefully reminiscent of Jimmy Durante, a popular entertainer of the time (although by 1961 Durante had been famous for decades). Durante, like Ben Grimm, was from a working-class New York background, and talked like it, saying things like "dis" and "dat." Durante passed away in 1980, so the Thing's dialect has long outlasted Durante. The other influence on the character of the Thing was his cocreator, Jack Kirby, who saw a lot of himself in the Thing. Ben Grimm was Jewish, like Kirby. However, it took a while for him to get there.

For the first forty-plus years of the Thing's existence, his religion was never expressly stated. Stan Lee has mentioned in the past that he never gave it any real thought, but that was not the case for

Kirby. He always considered the Thing to be Jewish, and, in fact, Kirby once portrayed the Thing wearing the traditional Jewish skull-cap and prayer shawl and holding a prayer book. The drawing hung in Kirby's home. After Lee and Kirby left the book, a few stories showed the Thing celebrating Christmas (and he appeared on the covers of various Marvel Christmas celebrations), but his religion was never specifically mentioned.

Finally, in 2002, in a fill-in issue of *The Fantastic Four*, writer Karl Kesel asked permission from editor Tom Brevoort to do a story about the Thing's past and expressly refer to his Jewish heritage. Brevoort consented, and the issue, *Fantastic Four #56*, was a lovely examination of the Thing's background (which echoed Jack Kirby's, right down to growing up on the Lower East Side of New York and a brother who died far too early, plus the Thing's name is Benjamin Jacob Grimm—the first name is Kirby's father's, and the middle name Kirby's birth name).

In the story, the Thing is protecting an elderly Jewish pawnbroker from a villain when, during the battle, the pawnbroker is injured. Not knowing what else to do, the Thing begins to pray the traditional Shema, the Hebrew confession recited at deaths. The pawn-

© Marvel Comics, image courtesy of Robert Means and Scott Morrison

broker survives but asks the Thing why he never told anyone about his religion. The Thing explains that the Jews have a hard enough time without everyone knowing that a monster like him is Jewish. It's a nice reminder of the tragic life of the Thing and the great humanity he contains within his monstrous exterior.

5

SPIDER-MAN

In *Amazing Fantasy* #15, the very last issue of the series, Peter Parker, the Amazing Spider-Man made his debut. Very quickly, he gained his own magazine, and soon after that, he was not only the single most popular Marvel character, but he was one of the most popular comic book characters period, rivaling the popularity of even Batman and Superman.

Amazing Fantasy #15 was written and drawn by Stan Lee and Steve Ditko, and the pair would team up to produce a notable thirty-eight-issue run of the ongoing *Amazing Spider-Man* title, during which time they would introduce pretty much every notable Spider-Man supporting character and villain, including Doctor Octopus, the Green Goblin, Aunt May, and J. Jonah Jameson.

The *Spider-Man* series was notable for the time because of how much of an everyman Peter Parker was—this was not some millionaire playboy, nor was he a successful reporter. He was a young adult trying to make his way in the world and failing as often as he succeeded. His trip to becoming a hero was filled with the sort of tragedy that makes great men. After being bitten by a radioactive spider, Parker gained remarkable abilities. Rather than use these powers for good, he first uses them to become an entertainer, and when a crook runs by him, chased by the police, Peter does nothing to stop him.

Later, however, he learns the folly of his ways when that same crook murders his beloved Uncle Ben. From that moment on, he resolves to use his powers for good, in honor of Uncle Ben's memory.

Spider-Man was soon popular enough to have both his own animated series (with a notable theme song: "Spider-Man, Spider-Man, does whatever a spider can") and be one of the first Marvel characters to receive a spin-off title. At one point in the 1990s, Spider-Man was juggling four monthly titles, a distinction shared only with Batman and Superman.

In 2002 Spider-Man made the leap to the big screen, in one of the most successful film franchises in movie history, setting box-office records with the first film that were broken by the second film. Currently, there are plans for a fourth Spider-Man film, although details have not yet been released.

AS TOUCHED ON earlier with the creation of Batman (see pages 33–34), sometimes identifying who should be considered the "creator" of a fictional character can be extremely difficult. If an editor tells a writer, "Write me a character involving turtles," and that writer creates Turtle-Man, who is the creator? Couple such loosely defined creatorship with an artist with an often poor memory and a bit of ill will, and you get a situation like Jack Kirby claiming that he and Joe Simon were the creators of Spider-Man.

Joe Simon and Jack Kirby had a long-lasting partnership, from their days at Timely in the 1940s, where they created Captain America, to their days at DC, where they produced one of the company's most popular wartime comics, *Boy Commandos*, to their independent days, when they cocreated the very first romance comic book. By the mid-1950s, however, comic sales had slowed to the point where it was not economically feasible for the two to shop themselves as a pair, so they split up, with Simon going to work in advertising and Kirby going to work at DC Comics.

The pair had one last hurrah, though, in 1959, when the publishers

at Archie Comics, just like Martin Goodman at Marvel Comics, saw
that DC was having success bringing back its superheroes. Archie
enlisted Simon to launch a line of superhero comics, and Simon
turned to his former partner for the project. Among the concepts
they worked on was a hero they had discussed a few years earlier
called the Silver Spider. The Silver Spider was a young boy who
wished upon a ring he found in a magical spider web and was transformed into the adult superhero the Silver Spider, who would fight
crime with a gun that would shoot webs (similar to the web shoot-
ers that Spider-Man wears around his wrists). At the time, Jack did
not like the name Silver Spider and suggested they use the name
Spider-Man. Simon even worked up a mock logo for the title. While
they abandoned the project then, they brought it back up when Simon was given the call from Archie to do the new line of superheroes. Ultimately, Simon would change the name of the character
to the Fly, but otherwise the concept stayed the same. Kirby drew
the series, which, like the other titles in the Archie line of superhero comics, did not last long (although the Fly did survive for
thirty issues).

Fast-forward a few years, and Stan Lee is looking for a teen superhero for Marvel Comics. He asks Kirby to come up with some
ideas, and Kirby remembers the Silver Spider/Spider-Man story and

pitches it to Lee. Lee is interested and asks Kirby to work up a proposal. Lee determined that the superhero Kirby came up with was too traditional, so he gave Kirby's proposal to Steve Ditko, who remarked to Lee that the premise sounded an awful lot like the *Adventures of the Fly* series from Archie. Lee concurred and asked Ditko to change it around, so Ditko eliminated the web gun, the costume, and the whole wishing-upon-a-ring premise, leaving the character as Peter Parker, the Spider-Man readers know and love.

So who created Spider-Man? After years of disputes with Marvel, Kirby at one point claimed that he created Spider-Man, but Kirby's memory was not always the greatest, and he would tend to go along with whomever he was talking to at the time. If the interviewer said something like, "So you created Spider-Man?" Kirby wouldn't contradict him. However, when asked about it later, Kirby clearly stated that he considered Ditko to be the man who developed Spider-Man. Stan Lee agrees, and ultimately, that is likely the fairest call, although it sure makes for an interesting argument.

AN INTERESTING ASPECT of the human memory is that it can often play tricks on us, making us remember hearing what we never actually heard. For instance, during the three seasons of the original *Star Trek* television program, Captain Kirk never says, "Beam me up, Scotty." Never in *Casablanca* does Rick tell Sam to "Play it again, Sam." We think we heard those phrases said, so we remember them being said. A similar situation occurs with *Amazing Fantasy* #15, which is famous for the quote from Peter Parker's Uncle Ben, "With great power, comes great responsibility." He never actually says it in the comic.

The phrase itself has an interesting history in the sense that no one has been able to determine definitively where Stan Lee came up with it. It is certainly possible that Lee came up with the line on his own, but is seems more likely that a line that classic was most likely taken from some older source. No one has yet definitively identified the quotation, although there have been many famous quotes that mirror the intent of the phrase, including Winston Churchill's "the price of greatness is responsibility." And presidents Franklin and Theodore Roosevelt both came close. Franklin: "Today we have learned in the agony of war that great power involves great responsibility." Theodore: "I believe in power; but I believe that responsibility should go with power."

In any event, while Peter credits this philosophy (which is the central theme behind his being Spider-Man) to his Uncle Ben Parker in later issues, and in the films the Uncle Ben character says it to Peter, Uncle Ben never actually says it in *Amazing Fantasy #15*. Instead, after Peter delivers Uncle Ben's killer to the police, as he realizes that Uncle Ben would still be alive had he acted responsibly in stopping the crook when he had the opportunity, Peter walks away while a caption box says: "And a lean, silent figure slowly fades into the gathering darkness, aware at last that in this world, with great power there must also come—great responsibility!"

© Marvel Comics

So Spider-Man learned this lesson in his first issue, but he did not learn it from his Uncle Ben.

* * *

ONE OF SPIDER-MAN'S greatest enemies is the Green Goblin, who is the main villain in the first Spider-Man film. The relationship between Spider-Man and Green Goblin is poignant—Spider-Man knows that the Green Goblin is Norman Osborn, father to his best friend, Harry, but neither Harry nor Norman know the truth (the split-personality Norman becomes the Green Goblin during psychotic breaks). It is an interesting dynamic, but a dynamic that Spider-Man cocreator Steve Ditko was strongly against.

When he debuted, the Green Goblin was a total mystery, even to the readers. This was not the first time that Stan Lee and Ditko had introduced a villain with a mysterious identity that was revealed after he had been a thorn in Spider-Man's side for a time. In the early 1960s, there was a mysterious villain trying to take over the New York mob. He was known only as the Big Man. Eventually, his identity was revealed to be Frederick Foswell, a reporter that Peter Parker knew from his job as a photographer for the *Daily Bugle*.

Ditko seemed to be fine with this revelation, but when it came time to reveal the secret identity of the Green Goblin, he and Lee disagreed vehemently over who the Green Goblin should turn out to be. Ditko argued that it simply did not make sense that the Green Goblin, a criminal with absolutely zero ties to Spider-Man before Spider-Man starts trying to keep the Goblin from committing crimes, would just happen to be someone that Peter knew in his real life. It was one thing for one criminal mastermind to be someone Peter knew personally, but another? Ditko felt that it strained the readers' suspension of disbelief to the breaking point.

Lee, on the other hand, felt that if you were going to spend the time to build up to revealing a major character's identity, you simply could not have it be someone who no one has ever seen before. Yes, it would be more realistic if Spider-Man pulled off the Green Goblin's mask and said, "Who are *you*?!" But since this is already a comic book where the hero dresses in red and blue tights and has powers like a spider, realism is not the main priority.

Whichever argument was more convincing, the point was made moot when Ditko left the title with *Amazing Spider-Man* #38. In the next issue, Green Goblin was revealed to be Norman Osborn.

STEVE DITKO'S DEPARTURE from *The Amazing Spider-Man* is one of comic's greatest mysteries while being at the same time not so much a mystery at all.

The mystery is, why did Steve Ditko leave *Amazing Spider-Man*? And it is considered a mystery because Ditko both (a) does not do official interviews and (b) has made statements in the past to the effect that his reasons are his own, and he won't tell anyone what they are. This was actually the basis for a recent BBC documentary by Jonathan Ross, which tried to get a definitive answer from Ditko on the topic. So yes, if not having a definitive answer from Ditko qualifies as something as an unsolved mystery, then this would be a mystery. However, there is enough information out there that Ditko's reasons for leaving are not really that mysterious. It is more a question of what specific straw broke the camel's back.

Ditko's experiences in many ways echoed Jack Kirby's on the *Fantastic Four*. In both cases, the attention in the media was spotlighted on Stan Lee more than it was on either Ditko or Kirby. This was partially because of Lee's engaging personality, partially because he was the editor in chief of Marvel and therefore more public of a personality, and partially because Lee was the one common element between the various notable creations. So it would appear that he was the *x* factor. As with Kirby on *The Fantastic Four*, as *Spider-Man* went on Ditko did more and more of the writing. In 1964, about a year and a half before quitting, Ditko made a bold request from Marvel that certainly seemed to highlight his displeasure with his current situation. He wanted credit as the plotter of the book; he wanted the extra money that would come from being at least the cowriter of the comic; and, most notably, he did not want to have to speak to Stan Lee at all. *The Amazing Spider-Man* was a good seller, so Marvel made the deal, but when one asks specifically not to have to talk to his cowriter/editor, it certainly does not bode well for his future on the title, does it?

Meanwhile, while Ditko and Lee were not speaking, Ditko was still consistently angry over Lee's writing for *Spider-Man*. Just as the two differed over how to handle the revelation of the Green Goblin's identity, Ditko was also upset over how Lee saw Peter Parker, period. Ditko was an objectivist, a follower of Ayn Rand, and he believed people were either good or evil, so he was bothered that Lee consistently portrayed Peter Parker as what Lee considered an "everyman," someone who had bad sides to his personality as well as good. Ditko wanted Parker to be a clearly defined good guy.

Around that same time, Stan Lee was purposely having Spider-Man guest star in the pages of *Daredevil* to see how artist John Romita would be able to handle Spider-Man if need be, so it is not as though Lee was not already planning for a world without Ditko.

Soon before Ditko quit, Marvel announced that it was releasing a series of animated television adaptations of its comics, and the cartoons would actually be roughly animated versions of the comic drawings. While Spider-Man was not part of this first wave of animated programs, it was clear that he would soon be featured on a television program too (and he was, the following year), so Ditko would be working on a book with a man he was angry at (to the point of not even speaking to him), in which he disagreed with how the main character was being portrayed, while also knowing that a character he helped create was most likely going to be turned into a television program from which he would not make any money.

Is it really a mystery, why he quit? Ultimately, it really does not matter what specific occurrence broke the proverbial camel's back—he clearly had more than enough reasons to quit.

* * *

As mentioned (see page 67), the Comics Code Authority had strangely strict guidelines for what was allowed in comics. Sometimes these seemed to run counterintuitive to the messages one might think people in positions of authority would want to deliver to children. Never was this more evident than with the story line for *Amazing Spider-Man* #96 through #98 in 1971.

In the early 1970s, the United States Department of Health, Education, and Welfare approached Stan Lee. It requested that he write a story line in *Amazing Spider-Man* addressing drug use. The department felt that *Spider-Man* (one of the highest-selling comics in the industry) would be an excellent platform for getting an antidrug message across to children. Lee was willing to go along with the request, but he was hamstrung by a simple rule set down by the Comics Code Authority: you could not have drug use in a comic, no matter how it was depicted. Marvel approached the Comics Code Authority with the information that they were specifically requested to do the comic by the U. S. government. However, the Comics Code Authority refused to bend on its position. In a bind, Lee approached

© Marvel Comics

Marvel publisher Martin Goodman and asked permission to bypass the Comics Code for this story line. Goodman approved, and for the first time since the code was created, a comic book appeared without its seal of approval.

While it was a big risk, and it could have led to the comic not being sold in a number of locations, the sales for the issue were fine, and Lee ultimately got more praise for it than criticism. This finally led the Comics Code Authority to overhaul its guidelines and

allow story lines with negative depictions of drugs.

Soon after the code overhaul, DC
did a story line in its team-up title
Green Lantern / Green Arrow with a dramatic drug-related plot. In the *Spider-
Man* story, Spider-Man's best friend,
Harry Osborn, has a problem with
pills. What sort of pills Harry was using, the reader does not know, but we
know that they're bad! In the *Green
Lantern / Green Arrow* story line, Green
Arrow's teen sidekick, Speedy (appropriate name, no?), is feeling neglected
by his mentor, so he turns to using heroin!

DC had its more dramatic story planned first, but DC editorial
did not want to run afoul of the Comics Code, so it held off on the
story. Then Lee's issues came out, and within a few weeks, the rules
were changed and DC was free to publish its story line. The book
proudly proclaimed on its cover that it was going to be about drugs,
while the *Spider-Man* issues gave no indication, save for the lack of
Comics Code approval on the cover.

THE AMAZING SPIDER-MAN comic strip, which is ostensibly written
by Stan Lee (whether it is ghostwritten is a whole different story)
and illustrated/cowritten by Stan's brother, Larry Lieber, is probably
the most successful superhero comic strip ever. It has been in print
since 1977, which is an impressive tenure during the days when adventure comic strips are a dying breed. Its circulation is not as high
as it once was, but it still appears in a number of papers. Luckily for
law-enforcement officials, though, it still ran in New Mexico newspapers in the late 1970s, where it inspired the invention of electronic
monitoring bracelets.

The idea of monitoring bracelets had been around for years in the world of animal tracking: scientists would clamp little ankle bracelets on to animals so they could keep track of their migration patterns. In the 1960s, some researchers at Harvard University considered the application of this technology to monitoring criminal offenders, but it did not get past the academic level. In a *Spider-Man* comic strip tale during the late 1970s, the villain Kingpin placed an electronic device on Spider-Man's ankle, which he used to monitor him. The strip writer (Lee, at that time) was certainly thinking of the bracelets they put on animals.

Well, a New Mexico district court judge, Jack Love, read the strip and theorized that such a device would work in real life as well. Love struck up an arrangement with Michael T. Goss, a former Honeywell computer salesman, who developed the devices. They were first tested in New Mexico in 1983. The tests went well, so they expanded the devices for use in Florida. These tests were also successful, and within six years, the devices had spread to a number of states. Nowadays, over one hundred thousand ankle monitors are used daily in the United States alone.

IN A RECENT story line in the *Spider-Man* comic book series, Peter Parker, who had been married in the comic books to Mary Jane Watson since 1987, had his marriage erased from existence by a supernatural character. Fans howled over the idea that simply because Marvel editorial felt Spider-Man should be a single hero they were willing to force the character to be single in the comic books (though he was married in the comic strip). However, most fans forget that the reverse happened in 1987 when Spider-Man was forced to get married despite the wishes of the comic book creative staff.

It is still disputed who came up with the idea, Stan Lee himself or Marvel editor in chief Jim Shooter. But in any event, one of the two came up with the idea that Peter Parker should marry his longtime sweetheart, Mary Jane Watson, in the *Spider-Man* comic strip, and

then, to make it a bigger deal, they
should coordinate the marriage with
the comic books and make a public-
relations sensation out of the wedding.

The problem in the comic strip was
that while Peter and Mary Jane had
dated in the past (Peter had even proposed in the late 1970s), Mary Jane
turned him down and left town. The
current *Amazing Spider-Man* comic book
writer, Tom DeFalco, had recently
brought Mary Jane back as a supporting cast member (along with the revelation that she had secretly known

Peter's identity as Spider-Man since they were both teenagers). But he
had even more recently written Mary Jane out of the book. So Mary
Jane not only had to make an abrupt return to New York in the comics,
she and Peter had to get back together and get engaged, in the span of
about three issues of the comic book, *Amazing Spider-Man* #290 through
292 (see pages 20–21 for the Superman
version of this story).

The end result was *The Amazing
Spider-Man Annual* #21 in 1987, which
was released at the same time that
The Amazing Spider-Man comic strip
was also featuring the wedding. In addition, a "wedding" was held at Shea
Stadium, before a New York Mets
game, between two actors dressed as
Spider-Man and Mary Jane. Stan Lee
was the justice of the peace presiding
over the ceremony.

So yes, twenty years later, Marvel
editorial determined it was going to

go the other way and have Spider-Man's marriage erased from existence, but it was only undoing the order imposed on it in 1987. Note that in the ongoing comic strip Peter and Mary Jane are still married.

VENOM, WHO WAS recently featured as the villain in the film *Spider-Man 3*, has an interesting lineage as a character. In the early 1980s, Spider-Man received a new black costume that turned out to be, in fact, an alien life form. The alien wanted to bond with Spider-Man, but the superhero managed to free himself of it. It sought out another host, ending up with a reporter named Eddie Brock whose career had been ruined when Spider-Man brought to justice a costumed villain that Brock had earlier identified as a different man entirely. The merged entity, calling itself Venom, became a frequent

rival of Spider-Man over the years (and so popular that he even gained his own title for a while).

However, things could have gone in a completely different direction if creator David Michelinie had gone with his original instinct, which was to make Venom a woman. The origins of the character would be fairly similar; it would still be someone who harbored a grudge against Spider-Man and would merge with the alien lifeform. Michelinie's original idea was to involve a pregnant woman who was rushing to the hospital with her husband to deliver her baby. They would be hailing a cab in the middle of New York while Spider-Man was fighting a super villain. A cab driver, distracted by the fight, would accidentally run over the woman's husband. He would die in front of her just as she goes into labor.

She would end up losing both her child and her sanity at the same time. After she got out of a mental institution, she would harbor an intense hatred for Spider-Man, making her a perfect host for the alien costume. When Michelinie pitched the idea to *Amazing Spider-Man* editor Jim Salicrup, however, Salicrup felt that readers simply would not believe that a woman could be the physical threat that Venom needed to be, even a woman with enhanced alien strength.

Michelinie went back to the drawing board, and the classic form of Venom was born.

AS MENTIONED, THE comic book story line about Spider-Man's new black costume turning out to be an alien and then becoming the new villain Venom was the centerpiece of the plot of *Spider-Man 3*.

It's interesting to note, however, that had it not been for a comic fan who never had a single comic book story published, the whole story line would likely never have existed.

In 1982 a young comic fan named Randy Schueller heard that Marvel was having some sort of competition for aspiring comic book writers and artists (the competition was published in 1983 as *The Official Marvel Comics Try-Out Book*), so he sent in a story idea. His concept was that Spider-Man would consider upgrading his costume, so he would go to Mr. Fantastic to help get a suit that was stronger than his cloth one. Along the way, he would decide to make the new costume all black. Marvel editor in chief Jim Shooter liked the idea enough to buy the story from Schueller for $220, and he would even allow Schueller the opportunity to write the story!

He assigned Schueller to Marvel writer-editor Tom DeFalco, who worked with the young writer for a couple of drafts of the story that ended up going nowhere. The story went to the scrap heap, and Schueller moved on with his life. Well, a year later Shooter was producing a major crossover starring all the Marvel superheroes, called *Secret Wars*. Shooter wanted to have a few notable changes happen to most of the characters (for instance, the Thing leaves the Fantastic Four and is replaced by She-Hulk), and remembering the black costume idea, decided that Spider-Man would get a new costume in the course of the series.

Spider-Man's new black costume was quite a sensation at the time, and, as mentioned, the revelation that the costume was actually an alien led directly to the creation of one of Spider-Man's most popular villains, Venom, who had his own series for almost four years and became the basis for a tremendously popular motion picture sequel.

All that for $220—quite a value!

IN 1998 TOM DeFalco introduced a new superhero, May "Mayday" Parker, known as Spider-Girl, the daughter of Spider-Man. She originally appeared in a *What If . . . ?* comic book (a Marvel title that explored various possible futures, like, "What if . . . Spider-Man had a daughter who grew up to become Spider-Girl?"), but Spider-Girl soon became the centerpiece of a whole line of comics (headed by DeFalco) depicting the sons and daughters of famous Marvel characters. Within a year or two, all the other titles in the line were canceled, leaving *Spider-Girl* as the only survivor. Surprisingly, the book kept going.

Spider-Girl flirted with cancellation a number of times, though, and ultimately, after around three years of publication, Marvel determined that the book would be canceled. Then something interesting happened: Marvel editor in chief Joe Quesada received a fan letter from a little girl, pleading with him not to cancel *Spider-Girl*, because there were so few superhero comic books for little girls to read, and *Spider-Girl* was her favorite. The idea that this particular comic appealed to a demographic that Marvel's other comics did not match added to the extremely heartfelt plea from the little girl (and a number of other *Spider-Girl* fans, who barraged Marvel with petitions to save the title), and caused Quesada to change his mind. Instead, Marvel would launch a new series of digests, reprinting older *Spider-Girl* stories, in an attempt to

reach this new market of girl readers. So *Spider-Girl* was saved! Quesada thought he would celebrate this achievement by visiting the little girl who wrote the letter.

The problem?

There was no little girl.

As it turned out, the letter from the little girl was actually written by an older male fan, who wrote it from the perspective of his infant daughter, feeling that everything the little girl said in the letter would be what his daughter would think if she were given the chance to read *Spider-Girl* when she was older. While presumably annoyed, this new bit of news did not affect the reprieve, and *Spider-Girl* is still being published today (the first series ended, and it was relaunched as *The Amazing Spider-Girl*), with the reprint digest selling particularly well.

6

THE INCREDIBLE HULK

The Incredible Hulk first appeared in late 1962 in the pages of *The Incredible Hulk*, written by Stan Lee and drawn by Jack Kirby. The concept was a simple Jekyll-and-Hyde tale. Scientist Bruce Banner is caught in an explosion of the gamma bomb he created, with the result that he becomes a violent, destructive green-skinned monster called the Hulk whenever he gets stressed or becomes angry. The army wishes to capture the Hulk, so Banner becomes a fugitive.

The series was quickly canceled (see page 119) and for a few years the hulk was the lead feature in the anthology *Tales to Astonish*, but in 1968 that book was retitled *The Incredible Hulk*, and the series has been published by Marvel Comics ever since, in varying forms.

In 1977 *The Incredible Hulk* television movie debuted, starring Bill Bixby as Bruce Banner and bodybuilder Lou Ferrigno as the Hulk. The movie was successful enough to lead to a series the next year. The series brought the character to new levels of popularity, and the show is still popular in reruns today. The series lasted until 1982, and spun off a number of made-for-television movies featuring the characters.

In addition to the live-action show and a number of animated television series, the Hulk also came to the silver screen in 2003, in a film directed by Ang Lee. A sequel, titled *The Incredible Hulk*, starring Ed Norton, was released in 2008.

THE HULK IS one of Marvel Comics' most popular heroes, so it is interesting to note that his original series was canceled after only six issues! A legend has been built around why Marvel canceled the series after six issues, but the most likely answer is relatively mundane.

The Incredible Hulk was replaced on the Marvel schedule with *Sgt. Fury and His Howling Commandos*, a war comic set during World War II and starring an elite team of soldiers. While Nick Fury has become a popular character in the Marvel Universe in his own right, he has never approached the same level of popularity as the Hulk, so it seems odd that the Hulk would be replaced by Fury's book, especially after such a short period. Stan Lee has created a legend regarding what happened, and it involved, surprisingly, a wager between Lee and Marvel publisher Martin Goodman!

The story goes that in 1963, running off a string of popular successes, Lee was riding high, but Goodman felt that the marketing of the comics using catchy titles like *The Amazing Spider-Man, The Fantastic Four, The Mighty Thor,* and *The Incredible Hulk,* was what was really selling the books. Lee countered that it was the strong work that he and Jack Kirby were doing, not the titles. Therefore the two agreed on a wager: Goodman would come up with the worst name of a book he could think of (and in a genre other than superheroes), and Lee and Kirby would have to create a new series based on that name. The pair ended the *Hulk* series to give Goodman's title, *Sgt. Fury* its place on Marvel's schedule.

Now, Martin Goodman never spoke on the topic (and has been dead since the early 1990s), so there is no definitive proof that Lee is misremembering what happened, but there are a few pieces on information that make Lee's version seem unlikely (not counting the fact that, as noted on pages 175–76, Lee made a plainly erroneous claim regarding his run writing *Sgt. Fury*).

First off, Jack Kirby had pitched the basic concept of *Sgt. Fury and His Howling Commandos* as a comic strip idea during the 1950s, so it seems hard to believe that Goodman happened to suggest a title that fit perfectly with a comic strip proposal Kirby had already made. Second, at the time DC had a popular series in *Our Army at War*, starring Sgt. Rock and Easy Company, a similar concept to Sgt. Fury, so it seems highly unlikely that Goodman would think Sgt. Fury was an absurd title and unpromising when Sgt. Rock was currently a popular series. Finally, there is the fact of the matter (as elaborated on pages 160–61) that Marvel was constrained in how many titles it was allowed to publish. So if it wanted to introduce a new title—and with the successes Lee and Kirby were having, they most likely wanted to keep trying to find new ones—some title had to come off the schedule. *The Incredible Hulk* was not a tremendous seller in its first six issues, so it would have made as much sense to replace it as anything else.

The Hulk, though, quickly made appearances in other titles, including becoming a founding member of the popular superhero team the Avengers. Jack Kirby has said that Marvel began receiving fan letters that suggested the Hulk was a bit of a cult classic, so Lee changed *Tales to Astonish* from a book starring Giant-Man to a book costarring Giant-Man and the Hulk (Hulk would eventually take over the entire series, with the book being retitled *The Incredible Hulk* in 1968).

ONE INTERESTING ASPECT of the way comic books are produced nowadays is that the majority of them are sold in the "direct market": that is, directly to the specialty stores on a nonreturnable basis. The guaranteed sale of a certain number of copies enables publishers to spend more money on the comic books. Before the direct market existed, comic book companies were forced to publish more comics than they actually sold, because retailers (mostly newsstands) were allowed to return the unsold copies. Therefore, even when sales were good (selling out 50 percent of the print run was considered good), the publishers were producing twice as many copies of any given issue than they actually sold. If it cost two cents to make a comic, it effectively cost four cents, since the company had to publish four copies to sell two (with the unsold copies simply being trashed). With this in mind, companies had to be as stingy as they possibly could, and under this system books had to be very popular for the comic company to turn a profit.

LATER (ON PAGES 212–13), I address another manifestation of this cost-cutting behavior: comic companies creatively retitling books to avoid having to pay additional registration fees with the post office. For the moment, though, let's focus on another symptom of cost-cutting—the coloring process. Nowadays, comic books are colored via computer, and printed on fairly expensive paper. This was not always the case. In the 1960s, Marvel Comics used standard four-color separations. Four-color separation is the easiest way to print colors. It entails taking four colors—cyan, magenta, yellow, and black—and layering them on top of one another, to seemingly create an infinite array of colors. Besides the simple coloring process, Marvel also used paper that was only slightly thicker than newsprint. This combination did not always bode well for certain color schemes. One color that caused trouble was gray.

It was not that comics could not use gray—they could. The problem was that the color combinations needed to make gray, coupled with the poor paper quality, resulted in an unstable color. If gray was used, it would not always look the same.

Therefore, when *The Incredible Hulk* #1 rolled around in 1962, Marvel had a problem. Dr. Bruce Banner is transformed into a monster called the Hulk by gamma radiation. The behemoth known as the Hulk is gray, but the gray proved to be inconsistent throughout the issue. Faced with this inconsistency, Marvel had to make a cost-effective decision. If gray would not print consistently, it would just have to be replaced with a color that would. That color was green. So, as of the second issue of *The Incredible Hulk*, the Hulk was green—the color he would maintain for the majority of his comic career.

Amusingly enough, after years of simply pretending that the Hulk was always green, when it came to referring back to the Hulk's origin (and Marvel went as far as to recolor the Hulk green when reprinting the original issue), later writers actually came up with a reason for why the Hulk was originally gray and then turned green. The gamma radiation, they explained, had not finished making its way through his body. Once it did, it made the Hulk completely green (although the gray look has returned at times over the years).

IN THE EARLY days of Marvel Comics, the writing staff was basically one man—Stan Lee. Lee occasionally had other writers do some work, including his younger brother, Larry Lieber, but for the most part it was Lee alone writing plots and, using the Marvel method, leaving it to the artists to figure out how to draw them. Then he would come in and write dialogue to fit the drawn pages. Lee simply did not have the time to write out full plots for all the books he wrote.

Not only was Lee writing a lot of comic books, but due to the amount of anthology/double feature books Marvel had, such as *Tales to Astonish*, Lee was also writing for quite a few characters. As a result, it was often difficult for him to remember characters' names. This is the genesis of the prominent use of alliterative names for Marvel characters. It is easier to remember names when the first and last names begin with the same letter, and Lee made great use of that trick, with characters such as Peter Parker, Reed Richards, Scott Summers, Warren Worthington, J. Jonah Jameson, Betty Brant, Sue Storm, and, of course, the alter ego of the Incredible Hulk, Bruce Banner.

However, even this did not always keep Lee from occasionally slipping up. One notable error occurred about two and a half years into Marvel's existence, when Lee began referring (for more than a couple of months) to the Hulk's other identity as Bob Banner rather than Bruce Banner, as he was originally named.

Responding to criticism of the goof, Lee, in issue #28 of *The Fantastic Four*, laid out how he was going to handle the situation, "There's only one thing to do—we're not going to take the cowardly way out. From now on his name is Robert Bruce Banner—so we can't go wrong no matter WHAT we call him!"

And that is still his official name today, although the television series ended up changing Robert to David. The reason why is an urban legend that will be addressed next.

THROUGHOUT THE HISTORY of adapting written works to film or television, there have always been differences between what fans of the original work have enjoyed and what the adaptor feels would best make for a good film/television series. Some notable examples include Dorothy's silver slippers becoming ruby ones in the film version of *The Wizard of Oz* and a different, considerably more optimistic, ending to the film version of *The Grapes of Wrath*. These changes occur even when the works being adapted are considered classic works of fiction. When the work in question is a comic book, you can imagine how little preference is given to the original story!

Such was the concern when writer-producer Kenneth Johnson began developing the comic book *The Incredible Hulk* as a television movie (with the intent of turning it into a regular series). Johnson began his television career working on the popular program *The Six Million Dollar Man*, and he was a producer and frequent writer for the spin-off of that show, *The Bionic Woman*.

At first Johnson was not interested in doing a show based on a comic book at all! In 1977 Universal Television gave him the chance to adapt for television any Marvel Comic property he wanted. Johnson initially turned down the offer, only reconsidering after rereading Victor Hugo's novel *Les Misérables*. The novel features a fugitive followed by a tenacious police officer. Johnson saw in the Hulk a chance to retell the *Les Misérables* story for a modern audience. The series featured Bill Bixby as Bruce Banner—on the run because of his monstrous alter ego, the Hulk—and Jack Colvin as Jack McGee, a tabloid reporter who is determined to track him down, echoing the way the steadfast police officer Javert in *Les Misérables* continues to track down the fugitive Jean Valjean.

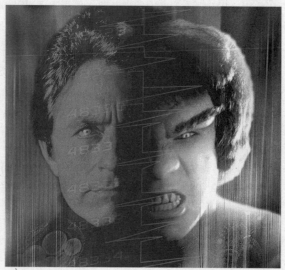

© Universal Studios

Beyond this basic concept, Johnson was not interested in holding true to the comic book series, so beyond the idea that Banner, on the run, turns into the Hulk when he is angry, the rest of the plot of the television series was completely different from the Hulk comic book. Johnson, as mentioned, even changed the name of the lead character from Bruce Banner to David Banner.

For years fans have wondered why exactly Johnson felt the need to change the name. The most prominent rumor was that Johnson felt the name Bruce sounded "too homosexual," and he wanted a stronger name for the character. Johnson has always denied this, and his stated reasoning follows with what we know about his development of the Hulk television property. Johnson thought that the general audience felt comic books were too childish, and the only way to appeal to an adult demographic was to make the series as adult as possible. He believed that alliterative names are a glaring sign of comic book heroes—that the very appearance of a name like Lois Lane, Peter Parker, or Bruce Banner would remind the audience that they were following a comic book character. So Johnson broke up the alliteration by changing Banner's name to David, while keeping Bruce as his middle name to at least throw the proverbial bone to the original fan base. (By the way, the first name Johnson chose to use instead was that of his son, David.)

While Johnson was able to change the name of the hero, he also wanted to change the very color of the Hulk! Johnson did not understand why the Hulk was green. The change from Bruce Banner to the Hulk is generally brought about by anger and rage, and Johnson thought that a character fueled by rage would naturally be red—the color that best represents rage, after all. He ended up asking Stan Lee why the Hulk was green, hoping to learn the motivation behind the color choice (was it meant to be a statement about envy?). Lee explained to him the story from earlier in this chapter (page 121), about the Hulk's color being determined due to poor color printing. Johnson, naturally, was disappointed that there was nothing more to the Hulk's coloring than a last-minute substitution due to a printing problem. Therefore, he pushed hard for the Hulk to be colored red on the television series. Ultimately, though, it was determined that the image of the Hulk as a green-skinned giant was just too great, and too firmly established, to change, so Johnson was left with a green Hulk.

Amusingly enough, in a 2008 relaunch of the Hulk comic book, writer Jeph Loeb introduced a new red Hulk into the comic, most likely as an allusion to Johnson's attempts to change the Hulk's color way back in the 1970s.

* * *

IT IS QUITE lucky that Kenneth Johnson was not involved in the production of the comic book *The Rampaging Hulk*, because then the rumors regarding his thoughts about the sexuality of Bruce Banner's name would have been given a whole new life.

The Rampaging Hulk was a black-and-white magazine that was set in the time between the cancellation of the Hulk's original series and the beginning of the Hulk's run in *Tales to Astonish*. Written by Doug Moench, the series was Marvel's attempt to cash in on the (at the time) new Hulk television series. The book did not sell particu-

larly well, and with #10 it was changed to *The Hulk!* with color stories designed to read just like the popular television series (which, due to the understandably small special-effects budget of weekly television, did not have nearly the same amount of action as a standard Hulk comic book).

Editor in chief Jim Shooter complained consistently that Moench wasn't writing stories that read like the television series (Moench does admit that he felt constrained by the restrictions of trying to write for a different medium—why use fewer special effects and action when he is not constrained by the budget of a television series?). Shooter ultimately decided that he would write an issue to demonstrate to Moench how it was done (Moench took the opportunity to just leave the series period), and the resulting issue was more than a bit controversial.

In the story, Shooter definitely matched the sort of gritty traveler feel that the television series had, but Shooter's attempt to add a touch of harsh reality also resulted in a rather unrealistic, and fairly offensive, situation. In *The Hulk!* #23, Banner is staying at a YMCA in New York. Shooter spends part of the story doing a nice job of depicting the grim world of sex workers and drug addicts, but all of that fine work is forgotten when Banner goes to the shower and two men attempt to rape him. When Banner escapes, one of the men exclaims, "Oh, pith."

A television executive called up Stan Lee to complain about the comic, and Marvel got a bit of negative media attention for a few weeks, but it ultimately blew over. Shooter today admits that the scene, or at least having one of the men say "Oh, pith," was a mistake, but he does not think the scene was offensive. Perhaps this story was where the Kenneth Johnson rumors started?

THE HISTORY OF aggressive trademark protection in comic books goes back to the 1940s, when DC Comics trademarked the name Superwoman as a preventative measure in case some other company tried to create a character with that name. Marvel Comics, though, was even more aggressive than that, constantly keeping its ear to the ground to hear if anyone was planning a project involving one of its trademarks.

For instance (as explained on pages 172–73), Marvel quickly rushed out a comic book starring a new character named Spider-Woman to maintain the trademark on the female derivation of its star hero Spider-Man. It did so after hearing of plans to produce a cartoon series starring a "Spiderwoman."

With the success of the television series *The Incredible Hulk* in the late 1970s, Marvel figured it was probably only a matter of time before the series would introduce a female counterpart to the Hulk. When a rumor came to the Marvel offices that that was exactly what the show was planning, Marvel acted quickly to introduce its own female derivation of the Hulk—the She-Hulk.

In early 1980, Marvel released *The Savage She-Hulk* #1, written by Stan Lee and drawn by John Buscema. The lead character was Jennifer Walters, cousin of Bruce Banner, who needed a blood transfusion after being shot by a criminal. Banner happened to be in town

that day, and with no other blood donors available, donated his radioactive blood, causing Walters to transform into the She-Hulk. This issue marked the last prominent Marvel superhero that Stan Lee was at least partially responsible for creating.

She-Hulk's series lasted only for a couple of years, but soon she popped up as a member of the superhero team the Avengers and also as a member of the Fantastic Four. In fact, she made superhero history in a way, as the first superhero to be members of two teams simultaneously! The character also appeared in the Hulk animated series, but never on the live-action program.

THE INCREDIBLE HULK was a popular television program that maintained a popular "cult status" in the late 1970s. The show was particularly popular with the male audience, making it unsurprising that the world of wrestling would attempt to tie in to the show's popularity.

Terry Bollea performed in a number of rock-and-roll bands over the years until, in the late 1970s, he was convinced to give professional wrestling a shot. After training for a period of time, Bollea made his pro wrestling debut in 1977, using his actual name. He adopted a number of other aliases, until he signed on with the World Wide Wrestling Federation (WWWF, later shortened to World Wrestling Federation, or WWF) in 1979, debuting as the Fabulous Hulk Hogan, the idea being that he was as strong as Lou Ferrigno, the bodybuilder who portrayed the Hulk on the television series.

The only problem with the name was that the WWWF did not clear the use of it with Marvel Comics. Naturally, when they were informed that a wrestler was calling himself the Hulk, Marvel warned the WWWF to stop or else it would pursue a legal claim against the wrestling group. The owner of the wrestling group, Vincent J. McMahon, chose instead to strike a deal, licensing the name from Marvel Comics.

This was the arrangement that Hogan worked under during his time at WWF, but it became an issue during the 1990s, when, after briefly retiring from wrestling in 1993, Hogan joined up with World Championship Wrestling (WCW), the main competitor to the World Wrestling Federation, in 1994. WCW picked up the licensing agreement with Marvel, but, possibly because Hogan had to kick in some of the fees himself, Hogan changed his name in 1996 to Hollywood Hogan.

Eventually, though, Hogan would return, both to the name Hulk Hogan, and to the WWF (now renamed World Wrestling Entertainment, or WWE). The WWE had a pair of new legal entanglements with Marvel. First, Marvel took issue with the use of the name in rebroadcasts of famous old matches by Hogan. This led to the WWE, for a time, going back and editing out any references to the name Hulk in past broadcasts and editing in the name Hollywood instead. Next, there was a problem over a character Hogan developed in 2003, dubbed Mr. America. Marvel felt this infringed upon its trademarked character, Captain America, in both the name and the costume (Marvel copyrighted Captain America's distinctive chest star, which also appeared on Mr. America's costume). It ceased to be an issue in 2003, when Hogan left the WWE.

In February 2005, Hogan solved the rights issue with Marvel once and for all, by purchasing from Marvel the right to call himself Hulk Hogan. This solved the rebroadcast problem. From now on, the WWE will have to go to Hogan himself if it wants to use his trademarked name.

READERS OF JULES Verne know how far in advance some of his ideas were. A number of inventions he mentions in his science fiction of the late 1800s eventually became real devices. For the most part, inventions from Marvel Comics have managed to be fantastical enough that they have not popped up in everyday life (although the attempt to reach the moon in *Fantastic Four* #1, published in 1961, seems at least plausible post Neil Armstrong). But surprisingly, one element from a Marvel comic that has turned up in real life is the gamma bomb that changed scientist Bruce Banner into the Incredible Hulk.

In 1961 Banner developed a gamma bomb for the U.S. government, which emitted gamma radiation rather than the destructive explosions that went along with nuclear bombs. This was how Banner was able to avoid being destroyed in the blast and was instead hit by enough gamma radiation to turn into the Hulk (remember, in comic books radiation = good) and also why the fallout was so small that the boy Banner saved (which is why he ran out to where the bomb was being tested) was unaffected by the radiation despite being nearby at the time.

In 2003 Stan Lee's idea was put into practice when the U.S. government revealed that it had developed a gamma bomb that worked by the same principles as Lee's device. The gamma bombs would not have the awesome destructive power of nuclear weapons but would emit energy that would be a great deal deadlier than conventional chemical explosives. The big difference is that rather than producing energy by triggering a nuclear fission or a fusion reaction, these bombs would just emit gamma rays that would kill through radiation or people breathing the radioactive particles from the ray emission. They would cut the fallout to a minimal level.

7

Captain America

There was already a notable patriotic superhero by late 1940 (MLJ Comic's the Shield), but no patriotic hero before or after caught the public's imagination like Joe Simon and Jack Kirby's Captain America. Debuting in December 1940, *Captain America Comics* #1 featured Captain America punching out Adolf Hitler on its cover, so while the United States did not enter the war for a year after the comic was released, it was clear even then how the public felt about Hitler and the Nazis—at least judging by the massive sales of *Captain America Comics* #1.

Steve Rogers was a weakling from New York who tried to enlist in the army but was declared 4-F. Still wishing to contribute, Rogers volunteered for an experiment involving a "Super Soldier Serum" that a government scientist had developed. When Rogers drank the serum, he transformed into the peak of human perfection, becoming Captain America. Along with his sidekick, Bucky, Captain America fought wartime saboteurs (led by the evil Nazi Red Skull) before the United States officially joined the war, at which point Cap joined the fight.

During the war, *Captain America Comics* was selling a million copies a month, but after the war, sales lagged and eventually the title was canceled. During Marvel's renaissance of superheroes in the early 1960s, it was only a matter of time before Lee would bring back Captain America, and in *Avengers* #4, in 1963, he finally returned. He would soon take over half of *Tales of Suspense* (Iron Man taking up the other half) and ultimately, in 1968, taking over the book entirely.

In 2008 Marvel stunned its fans when it had Steve Rogers seemingly murdered in his comic, courtesy of an evil plot masterminded by his archnemesis, the Red Skull. Rogers's former sidekick, Bucky, has recently taken on the title of Captain America.

CAPTAIN AMERICA STARRED in an animated series during the 1960s and a poorly received film in the late 1980s. Currently, a new Captain America film is in development, with a possible 2010 release.

In 1940, with the war raging in Europe, there was an increasing mixture of national pride and anti-Nazi sentiment in the United States, so it was inevitable that a company would introduce a superhero that would appeal to both demographics, and that's what MLJ did in 1940 with the Shield. MLJ was a comic company formed by Maurice Coyne, Louis Silberkleit, and John Goldwater in 1939 (the name of the company took the first initials of each man) and produced a number of superheroes that did not last long, but for a time, the Shield was popular, starring not only in the anthology *Pep Comics* but also his own book, *Shield-Wizard Comics* (starring another MLJ superhero, the Wizard).

The Shield was Joe Higgins, the son of a scientist who develops a chemical that gives him super strength and invulnerability. Wearing a red, white, and blue triangular chest plate that looks like a shield, Higgins goes to work for the FBI, fighting against saboteurs and foreign spies.

Louis Silberkleit ran a pulp magazine company in the 1930s. Timely publisher Martin Goodman got his start in the pulp business working with Silberkleit, and Goodman and Silberkleit maintained a friendly relationship even after Goodman left to start his own pulp magazine company.

When Joe Simon and Jack Kirby brought Captain America to Martin Goodman, they knew they had something special, so they

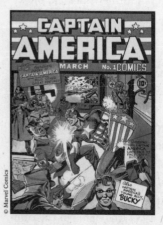

asked Goodman for a cut of the profits of the comic, and Goodman agreed. There was so much buzz about the character that they skipped the normal step of introducing the character in an anthology and gave him his own title right off the bat.

However, when the folks at MLJ heard the buzz about Captain America, and saw the character, they took issue with the appearance of the character. Captain America carried a triangular shield that looked quite similar to the Shield's chest plate. Since they were friendly, Silberkleit did not pursue legal action but rather told Goodman that MLJ objected to the design and wanted Timely to change Captain America's shield. Good-

man quickly agreed, and Simon and Kirby quickly designed a new round shield that debuted in the second issue of the series.

The round shield went on to become one of the most notable aspects of the Captain America series, so MLJ ended up doing Timely a favor in asking it to change the shield!

MLJ, by the way, while not having great success with superheroes, debuted a young teenager as a backup humor story in the Shield's series *Pep Comics*, Archie Andrews. Archie soon bumped the Shield from the top spot in *Pep Comics*, and within a year's time, the entire company was renamed Archie Comics.

WHILE CAPTAIN AMERICA was a gigantic smash as soon as his first issue was released, not everyone in the United States was a fan of the comic. Remember, the first issue was released a full year before the United States went to war with Nazi Germany, and while most Americans were anti-Nazi, there were still a number of pro-Nazi supporters in the country, and they were not happy with a comic book created by two Jewish men whose first two issues had the title character punching out Adolf Hitler.

Joe Simon recalls one specific group that was irate over Captain America, the German American Bund. This was a pro-Nazi group that was heavily financed and used its riches to espouse its support of the Third Reich. It organized pseudomilitary training camps in Long Island and held huge rallies at places as large as Madison Square Garden in New York City. The group organized a deluge of hate mail to the Timely offices, along with obscene telephone calls with threatening messages. Simon recalled that they did not take it seriously at first, but when groups of menacing-looking men began to gather in front of the Timely offices on Forty-second Street, their attitudes changed. They reported the threats to the police, and soon they were assigned police protection.

One day, not long after the police protection began, a phone call came into the Timely offices. It was none other than the mayor of New York, Fiorello La Guardia, who wanted to talk to the editor of *Captain America Comics*.

La Guardia is famous in New York history for reading the newspaper funnies over the radio to the city's youngsters when there was a newspaper strike in 1945. So it is not that surprising that he would take an interest in a comic as popular as *Captain America* was at the

time, but, still, when you go to
work at your comic book company, you don't expect to get a
phone call from the mayor of
New York!

Simon picked up the phone,
and La Guardia, known as the
Little Flower, said to him, "You
boys over there are doing a good
job. The city of New York will
see that no harm will come to
you." As a creator, it does not
get any better than that.

WHEN IT COMES to avoiding getting taken advantage of in a business
arrangement, it is always advisable to get the terms of the deal written down on paper. Joe Simon and Jack Kirby knew that they could
not trust a verbal arrangement with Timely publisher Martin Goodman over royalties, so they had Goodman sign a written contract
stating that he would pay Simon and Kirby a 15 percent share of the
profits of *Captain America*'s success, but that agreement quickly appeared to have been filed under the category of "empty promises."
Goodman claimed that he was glad to share the profits with Simon
and Kirby, and he did pay them their 15 percent, but that 15 percent
was based on a remarkably low profit. Goodman was presumably
using some creative accounting to come up with the argument that
he was barely turning a profit on a comic book that was, at its peak,
selling a million copies a month.

As a result, although Simon and Kirby were being paid well in
their salaried positions at Timely, they felt like they could negoti-
ate a better deal at DC Comics, where they would not be taken
advantage of in the same manner. And the deal they signed with
DC did end up paying them quite well for the next few years. How-

ever, with their departure, the paltry royalties they had received from Timely turned into zero royalties—Goodman ceased paying them.

Years later, in 1967, Joe Simon pursued taking control of the copyright of Captain America when it was first up for renewal. He attempted to challenge the copyright of Timely (by then Marvel Comics) by asserting that he delivered Captain America, not as a work-for-hire comic, but as an independent worker, and that he should gain the benefit of the second term of the copyright. Kirby had already settled with Marvel by that time, so Marvel was assured half of the copyright. Still, Simon kept fighting until he, too, ultimately settled in 1969.

While Simon was investigating in preparation for a possible trial, he found some bizarre financial information regarding Captain America. One of the events that really galled Simon was when Captain America received his own film serial in 1944.

The serial starred Dick Purcell, and it was so drastically different from the comic book that one would almost wonder if they had not simply added Captain America into the plot of an entirely different film. For years Simon was haunted by the idea that his cocreation was the star of a film, and he was to receive no money for it! So he was quite surprised to find out, in 1967, that Martin Goodman had received zero dollars for Republic Pictures' license to Captain America for the film serial. Goodman felt that having a film released of Captain America would pay for itself in terms of added publicity, and while it certainly is possible to quantify the value of publicity when it comes to monetary damages, it is still striking that Goodman did not receive a single red cent for the adaption of one of the most popular comic books at the time.

AFTER JOE SIMON and Jack Kirby left Timely, a young staffer was placed in charge of *Captain America* (except for a three-year span when he was in the military), but young Stan Lee was at a loss. Now that

World War II was over, Captain America did not exactly have much in the way of a purpose anymore. He was designed to fight the Nazis, but with the Nazis finished, what else could Captain America do?

At first Captain America returned stateside, and Steve Rogers became a teacher. Captain America and Bucky began fighting crime like ordinary superheroes. Eventually, Bucky was shot, and Captain America got a new sidekick, Steve's girlfriend, Betsy Ross, who took to calling herself Golden Girl. By now it was the late 1940s, and the book's sales continued to fall. For the last couple of issues, the format changed to include horror stories as well as Captain America stories, and the book was renamed *Captain America's Weird Tales*. In the last issue, Captain America did not even appear in his own comic book!

That looked like it for Cap, but for a brief period in the 1950s, while the company was calling itself Atlas, it decided to give superheroes a try. Perhaps it thought the name change might have had some impact. In any event, Captain America returned, ultimately in his own magazine once again. Only this time, with the Nazis gone, Captain America had a new target.

The covers of the first issues of the return of Captain America proudly state on the cover (and this is the actual cover tagline), "Captain America . . . Commie Smasher,"

and so began a short-lived revival where Captain America would take on the evil Reds for a time before sales became just too low to continue. These issues were drawn by a young John Romita, who would later go on to have great success at Marvel and to serve as its art director for years.

When Marvel brought Captain America back for good in the early 1960s, it changed his story so that he was left for dead at the end of World War II after a rocket explosion left him stuck in suspended animation in the middle of the Arctic. Bucky was presumed to have died in the same rocket explosion, but recently Bucky was revealed to have survived the explosion as well). All the "Commie smasher" stories were explained away in the modern comic to have been other people posing as Captain America and Bucky.

ONE OF THE most underappreciated jobs at comic book conventions is that of the actors who dress up as superheroes and endure hours of humiliation simply to entertain comic book fans. Usually, they are not exactly the most talented actors in the world, although in the late 1970s in New York, the actor portraying Captain America at comic conventions was none other than *Star Trek: The Next Generation*'s Jonathan Frakes!

Frakes had moved to New York after studying theater at Penn State and Harvard. While in New York, he was a member of the acting company the Impossible Ragtime Theater and appeared in plays or bit roles on television, but acting roles were not plentiful at the time for Frakes. During this acting dry spell, he took on a number of other jobs to make ends meet, working as a waiter and a furniture mover, but the most memorable part-time job he took was appearing at comic book conventions as Captain America, in full costume.

Frakes took the role seriously and was an excellent Captain America, putting up with the fans and their questions with grace and aplomb.

Frakes eventually moved to Los Angeles, where he began to get better acting roles, appearing as a guest on a number of television series over the next few years, as well as starring roles in some failed pilots. Eventually, in

1987, Frakes would land the role that has made him famous to this day, that of Commander William Riker on *Star Trek: The Next Generation*.

Undoubtedly, Frakes has used his experiences appearing at comic book conventions as Captain America to inform his appearances as himself at Star Trek conventions, and, in fact, Frakes is known for being an excellent guest at conventions, extremely friendly and accommodating to fans. Perhaps some of the best qualities of Captain America rubbed off on him while he was wearing the suit.

THE 1970S WERE an interesting time at Marvel Comics, as well, particularly for the books written by Steve Englehart. In the early 1970s, Stan Lee was taking on more and more business-related dealings on top of his being Marvel's editor in chief, so he could no longer manage to write his titles. Thus Roy Thomas and Gerry Conway more or less split the books up, with Thomas notably getting *Fantastic Four* and Conway getting *Amazing Spider-Man*. Eventually, when Lee was promoted to publisher of Marvel, he named Thomas the editor in chief. This resulted not only in Thomas leaving a number of books because of his added responsibilities but also in the loss of Conway, as he was hoping to be named editor in chief and did not want to stay at Marvel if Thomas was going to be the new editor in chief instead (though not due to any personal enmity toward Thomas). This opened up a number of titles to new writers, and that is where Steve Englehart stepped in, taking over a number of prominent titles such as *The Avengers* (from Thomas) and, most notably, *Captain America* (from Conway).

The young Englehart (in his midtwenties at the time) had many of the same views that Marv Wolfman and Len Wein had at DC Comics in the late 1960s (as detailed on pages 66–68), except that Marvel actually gave Englehart the freedom to try out his ideas. As he took on Captain America, he introduced ideas of pacifism and antiwar protest into the title while still maintaining a fairly traditional superhero-fighting-super-villain style to the comic, which was highlighted in his epic Secret Empire story line, where the villain was none other than the president of the United States!

Captain America and his partner at the time, the Falcon (one of the very first prominent African American superheroes), were caught up in an elaborate plan by the villainous group the Secret Empire, which attempted to ruin Captain America's reputation and take control of the world. The story line was set during the days of Watergate, and a lot of the Secret Empire's rhetoric was designed to resemble Nixon's administration in the way he attempted to keep a veil of secrecy over his White House. Ultimately, Englehart moved from subtle commentary to overt commentary, when Captain America tracked down the leader of the Secret Empire, Number One, and he turns out to be the president of the United States! At the last moment, Englehart decided not to show the actual face of Nixon in the issue, but the dialogue makes it clear that it is, indeed, supposed to be Nixon. The president, wracked with guilt over his role in the Secret Empire, then commits suicide.

While it is hard to imagine in this day and age, at the time Englehart claims he was not told once by an editor to tone down his story, and the decision to avoid actually showing Nixon's face was simply self-censorship on his part. Whenever there is a controversial story line in comics today, it is always helpful to imagine trying a story like Englehart's in the current context, and suddenly the modern stories do not seem quite so controversial.

ANOTHER EXAMPLE OF a modern story being one-upped by a story from the past involves Jean Marc DeMatteis's run as writer of *Captain America* during the early 1980s, when DeMatteis planned on killing off Captain America twenty years before Marvel decided to do it!

DeMatteis began writing the title in 1982. Paired with artist Mike Zeck, DeMatteis's run was well received. During his run, DeMatteis brought back Bucky from the 1950s (the "Commie

smasher"–era Bucky), Jack Monroe, and turned him into an interesting supporting cast member, Nomad.

While the title was nearing its three hundredth issue, DeMatteis
developed a bold new approach to Captain America that he proposed and his editor, Mark Gruenwald, accepted. DeMatteis was
going to have Captain America announce that he was going to try to
go about making the world a better place without using violence.
This, of course, would be taken as bizarre news by the rest of the
world. Captain America would begin to lose popular support as he
traveled around to discuss pacifism. Ultimately, Jack Monroe would
be manipulated by the bad guys into thinking that Captain America
was out to hurt America, and Monroe would end up assassinating
Captain America at a rally.

At this point, DeMatteis was planning to replace Captain America with Black Crow, a Native American superhero that he had introduced earlier in his run writing
the book.

DeMatteis was to begin the
story line in a double-size #300,
which was already written, but
then Marvel editor in chief Jim
Shooter discovered the plans,
and he quickly shut them down,
overruling Gruenwald's earlier
approval.

Shooter then cut the size of
#300 down to a regular comic
and rewrote the issue himself.
DeMatteis took the cue to quit
the title. Eventually, Gruenwald
would end up taking over the
book himself, writing it for an
amazing eight years!

8

THE X-MEN

The *X-Men* debuted during the same month in 1963 as another notable Marvel team book, the Avengers (both titles were by Stan Lee and Jack Kirby). The X-Men were a team of mutants, humans born with a different genetic makeup that manifests itself at puberty in the form of superhuman powers. With the public fearful of them and with the need to train these young mutants in how to control their powers, Professor Charles Xavier (aka Professor X) formed a school for mutants and taught his students, not only how to use their powers, but how to use them to fight the forces of evil as the superhero team known as the X-Men. The first team of students was made up of Cyclops, Marvel Girl, Iceman, Angel, and the Beast. Their biggest nemesis was Magneto, who led the Brotherhood of Evil Mutants, a group that wants to either destroy or dominate normal humans. Later on, Magneto and Professor X would come to represent the Malcolm X/Dr. Martin Luther King dynamic when it came to the rights of mutants.

After a few years, the original *X-Men* series was canceled, and Marvel just published reprints for a number of years, until editor in chief Roy Thomas suggested that writer Len Wein and artist Dave Cockrum introduce a new team of X-Men. This "All-New,

All-Different" team of X-Men consisted of international mutants such as Wolverine (Canada), Storm (Kenya), Nightcrawler (Germany), Banshee (Ireland), and Sunfire (Japan), plus an Apache mutant called Thunderbird. After debuting in *Giant-Size X-Men* #1, the new team (led by Cyclops, the lone original member to remain) took over the X-Men title with *X-Men* #94.

Writer Chris Claremont scripted Len Wein's plots and soon took over the writing of the book himself. Artist John Byrne replaced Cockrum with *X-Men* #108. Claremont and Byrne worked together for the next three years on a dynamic run that was highlighted by the character Wolverine becoming one of the most popular characters in all of comics, and their depiction of the former X-Man, Marvel Girl, who gained fantastic powers (and a new name, Phoenix) that ultimately drove her mad, causing her to choose to sacrifice herself rather than endanger the universe. By the end of the "Dark Phoenix Saga," Claremont and Byrne had taken a title that was not even being released monthly and turned it around so much that, by the time Byrne left the title after *Uncanny X-Men* #143, the book was poised to become Marvel's best-selling comic.

The next year, it achieved that distinction, a position it has held for most of the last twenty-five years. Claremont wrote the book for a remarkable seventeen-year run, seeing it expand from one poor-selling title to an entire line of X-Men-related comic books.

During the 1990s, the X-Men starred in the popular and long-running animated series titled *X-Men*. In 2000 they starred in a second animated series, *X-Men: Evolution*, which was a success as well, running for four seasons. Also in 2000, the first X-Men film was released to great popular success. Two blockbuster sequels followed, with more movies in the works, including a Wolverine spotlight film and a Magneto spotlight film.

IN 1971 ROOMMATES Gerry Conway and Len Wein were writing for Marvel Comics and DC Comics, respectively (although both would switch back and forth a number of times during the decade). During this time rooming together, within months of each other, Conway debuted Man-Thing (based on a plot by Roy Thomas), a green misshapen monster who lives in a swamp, and Wein debuted Swamp Thing, a green misshapen monster who lives in a swamp.

Both men deny that they knew what the other one was working on, and it is believable because both men were aware of a 1940s character called the Heap, who was a green misshapen monster who lived in a swamp.

Like Neil Gaiman and J. K. Rowling (see pages 74–75), the two men most likely just shared the same influences. This is notable when taking into consideration the debut of the Doom Patrol and the X-Men.

The Doom Patrol first appeared in 1963, in DC's *My Greatest Adventure* #80. The X-Men first appeared a couple of months later in *X-Men* #1. Like the mutant X-Men, the members of the Doom Patrol are all unable to fit normally into society anymore. They are all notable celebrities who were transfigured in acidents, like racecar

Page from *Airboy Comics*, vol. 10, no. 3,
by Ernest Schroeder.

driver Cliff Steele, who awoke after a fiery crash to learn that his brain had been transferred into a robot! Both books are about misfit superheroes that are not accepted by society and are led by a brilliant man in a wheelchair (Dr. Niles Caulder for the Doom Patrol and Dr. Charles Xavier for the X-Men).

Doom Patrol creator Arnold Drake certainly believes that the X-Men were based on his creation, even though for Stan Lee to use his idea he would have had to have heard about it well before the Doom Patrol made its debut, given the amount of time needed for

© DC Comics © Marvel Comics

the production of the comic. Drake felt that it was extremely possible that some staffer told Lee about the project.

Admittedly, Drake's scenario is probable, as there was often communication between the companies, especially back in the days when almost everyone involved lived either in New York City or its outskirts.

However, the X-Men are not so similar to the Doom Patrol to make Drake's claim convincing. There are many more dissimilarities than there are similarities. And the similarities that do exist are not the most original of ideas. Reluctant superheroes? The Thing from the Fantastic Four had already that down pat. *The Fantastic Four* also has its own professor type, who happens to stretch, just like Elasti-Girl, one of the original members of the Doom Patrol.

So while Arnold Drake went to the grave believing that X-Men was ripping off his Doom Patrol, there is not enough evidence to give his claim that much merit, although the coincidence is certainly an amusing one.

* * *

As mentioned (on pages 67–69), the Comics Code Authority at one point had overly strict guidelines for what was allowed in the comics. Often, as described on the aforementioned pages, the comic book creators would enjoy having some fun with the strict rules, which is certainly the case for Neal Adams and Roy Thomas during their run creating *X-Men*. The two men did not work on the book together for that long, only about six issues in total, but they are well remembered

by fans. During their run, they introduced a new X-Men villain named Sauron. Sauron is a mutant who transforms into a pterodactyl-like creature and can hypnotize people and drain their "life force."

What Sauron really was, was an attempt by Adams to get around the Comics Code ban on vampires. Vampires aren't allowed? Okay, then the X-Men will face a mutant who transforms into a flying creature, hypnotizes people, and sucks the "life force" out of them.

A similar situation occurred in the pages of *Amazing Spider-Man*, but in that case it was Stan Lee taking advantage of the relaxation of the Comics Code (see pages 109–11). As soon as vampires were technically allowed to be used in comics, Lee wanted Roy Thomas to get together a vampire character as soon as humanly possible, and within a couple of weeks of the guideline changes, Thomas had created Morbius the Living Vampire, who first fought Spider-Man then later became somewhat of an ally.

Readers often make the mistake of thinking that Morbius was also an attempt to get around the rules (that is, the rules that forbade vampires) with a sort of linguistic trick: the rules did not say

anything about *living* vampires! But
that was not the case. Lee and Thomas wanted a character they could
theoretically turn into a protagonist,
so they wanted to differentiate him
from a typical vampire. It is under-
standable, though, considering the
turnaround time for the creation of
Morbius was so short, that it appears
as though they were going to create
him before the Comics Code changes
went into effect. That is not the case.

NIGHTCRAWLER WAS ONE of the most interesting new characters in
Giant-Size X-Men #1. A German, Kurt Wagner, had the appearance
of a demon but in reality was a jovial mutant who was very much a
religious person. He was also a teleporter who fancied himself a
swashbuckler, since he grew up idolizing the films of Errol Flynn.
Wein and Cockrum, and later Claremont especially, did a wonderful job twisting the stereotype of the
evil-looking character. As great of a
character as Nightcrawler is, X-Men
fans almost missed out on having
him as a member of the team, because Dave Cockrum originally intended for him to be a DC Comics
character!

Cockrum came to the X-Men from a
stint on DC Comics' *Legion of Superheroes*, a comic about a group of young heroes in the distant future. Cockrum was
one of the more creative artists working
in comics during the 1970s and '80s,

© DC Comics, Image courtesy of Glen Cadigan and Scott Rowland

and he was constantly creating new characters that he wanted to use in his comics. During his time on *Legion*, he pitched DC a variety of new characters as well as a spin-off book about a group called the Outsiders.

The Outsiders was going to be a team of heroes that were not accepted into the Legion of Super-Heroes, but still operated in the same time period as the legion but as an unofficial team. Nightcrawler was going to be one of the members of the team, without any real difference in his appearance at all (although presumably, he would not have been German in the Outsiders).

Luckily, DC editor Murray Boltinoff felt that Nightcrawler was too funny looking, so Cockrum was able to bring Nightcrawler to the X-Men, where he has remained a popular member for thirty-plus years.

ANOTHER X-MAN WHOSE genesis was in Cockrum's Outsiders pitch is Storm. In the *X-Men* comics, Storm is Ororo Munroe, the daughter of an American photojournalist and a Kenyan princess who lost her parents during the Suez War when a fighter plane crashed into her family home. Ororo survives the disaster, but while covered in rubble she develops deep claustrophobia. When Professor Xavier finds her, she is living in the deserts of Africa, where the people are worshipping her as a goddess, because she is using her mutant ability to control the weather to bring them rain.

The creation of her character, though, was a good deal more complicated than that. She was born out of, not one, but five separate designs Cockrum had done in the past. Storm's main look is based on a combination of two other proposed Outsiders, Trio and Quetzal. Cockrum and Wein decided to merge those two designs with a third proposed Outsider character, Black Cat, who could shape-shift into a cat. Then they decided that shape-shifting into a cat was not impressive enough, so they merged the visual for this new Trio/Quetzal/Black Cat character with the powers of a fourth proposed character, Typhoon, who could control the weather. Finally, Cockrum had done some design work on X-men, and he took a few aspects of his early redesigns for Marvel Girl's costume (including a cape) and added them to the hybrid character. The end result was Storm, who is one of the most famous members of the X-Men, particularly due to being heavily featured in the X-Men films, in which she is played by Halle Berry.

ONE OF THREE new X-Men who made appearances before *Giant-Size X-Men* #1 (Banshee and Sunfire were the other two), Wolverine first turned up in the pages of *The Incredible Hulk* #181, where Wolverine fights against the Hulk on behalf of the Canadian government. Wolverine is a scrappy little fighter (he stands about five foot three) who has unbreakable metal claws and the ability to heal from injuries. Wein came up with the character when he wanted Hulk to fight a Canadian-inspired character, and after doing some research, Wein discovered that wolverines, who keep mostly to Canada, have the tenacity and fighting spirit you expect from a proper superhero.

When he took over from Len Wein, Chris Claremont followed Wein's plot directions for most of the characters. Wein did not put too detailed a plan into place for the characters, since no one knew if the book would be popular enough to keep from being canceled. But one character Claremont took in a substantially different direction was Wolverine, who Wein wanted to be, surprisingly, an actual wolverine!

A reoccurring character in a number of Marvel books during the 1970s was the High Evolutionary. The most prominent geneticist in the Marvel Universe, he often lets his genetic experimenting take him over to the point where he acts as if he is a godlike creator of beings. His base of operations is on Wundagore Mountain. He mutated a number of animals into serving as his personal bodyguards, the Knights of Wundagore.

Originally, Wein planned for Wolverine to be one of High Evolutionary's subjects, a mutated wolverine that escaped and now thinks he is a man. Wein gave clues to this effect in his early issues of the series. In *X-Men* #98, a technician gets a reading on Wolverine that suggests he is not a full-fledged mutant. In addition, Wolverine's claws were intended by Wein to be gloves he wore rather than part of his skeleton. They were to be retractable claws that would telescope out and retract back into the casings of the glove.

Wein also intended for Wolverine to be a teenager like the rest of the new X-Men, but he was always drawn with his mask on in his early appearances in *Hulk* and *X-Men*, and when Dave Cockrum finally drew him without a mask on, he looked clearly older than the other X-Men. Wein would note at the time, "You just put thirty years on that guy," but the new look lasted.

Check out (on page 173) which Marvel superheroine ended up inheriting Wolverine's unused origin.

WHEN WOLVERINE BEGAN on the team, he was mostly a background character. Wein saw his personality as being like a wolverine, so he'd be irritable and always wanting to fight. Wein used this type of personality to play Wolverine off of his teammates, as the guy who irritates everyone. When Chris Claremont and Dave Cockrum sat down to plan out their run, each man seemed to have a favorite character: Claremont's was Nightcrawler, while Cockrum had an affinity for Colossus, the quiet Russian gentle giant who could

transform into superstrong and invulnerable "living steel." When Wein and Cockrum were laying out *X-Men*, their intent was for Colossus to be the star of the comic, which is why he was given a costume that is made up of primary colors such as yellow and red. Whoever the star of the *X-Men* was, it sure wasn't Wolverine. That is, until John Byrne joined the title. But what drew Byrne to Wolverine? The answer was as simple as Wolverine's nationality.

John Byrne was born in England, but when he was a child, his family immigrated to Canada, which is where Byrne grew up. So when he took over from Cockrum as the artist for *X-Men*, he knew that Cockrum and Claremont both had their favorite characters, so he chose the short Canadian fellow as his personal project.

Byrne specifically spotlighted the dark side of Wolverine (in one early issue in the Claremont-Byrne run, Wolverine kills an enemy guard instead of simply wounding him—it seems quite commonplace nowadays, but at the time it was a bold thing to show a character killing without being absolutely forced to). Soon the character was becoming more and more popular. The story featured in *X-Men* #132 and #133 was probably the clincher.

In that story, the X-Men are held captive by the evil Hellfire Club. In a battle with the Hellfire Club, Wolverine is smashed through the ground, into the sewers, and left for dead. The Hellfire Club proceeds to capture the rest of the team members. The issue finishes on a cliff-hanger. There is a spotlight on the sewer, and the reader sees a hand pop out of the muck. It is Wolverine, and the final panel is a beautifully illustrated view of the badly beaten Wolverine looking up to the sky (his body and face covered in shadows from the grates) and shouting, "Okay suckers—you've taken yer best shot! Now it's my turn!"

In the next issue, he rescues the X-Men and kills a good many Hellfire Club guards in the process. That story line most likely cemented Wolverine's popularity, but, just to make one last addition before he left, Byrne gave Wolverine a new dark brown and tan costume before he departed *Uncanny X-Men* to take over *The Fantastic Four*.

CHRIS CLAREMONT AND John Byrne had been developing a story line involving one of the X-Men, Jean Grey, for a long time. In *X-Men* #100, Jean Grey seemingly sacrifices her life to pilot a space shuttle to Earth with the rest of her teammates. But in the next issue, when it crashes she emerges as the Phoenix. She apparently had tapped into some deep reserve of power within her mind and was now much more powerful than she had ever been before.

For the next couple of years, she seems like the same Jean Grey that everyone knew before, but, eventually, an illusionist mutant named Mastermind slowly breaks down her mental barriers and appears to turn Jean to the dark side, making her a member of the Hellfire Club. Jean breaks free of this, but slowly but surely darker aspects of her personality begin to surface, and eventually she begins to see herself as a separate personality, the Dark Phoenix. The power is too much for her mind to handle, and she flies into outer space and devours an entire sun, destroying a planet of aliens. She returns to Earth, and the X-Men face off against her and, ultimately, using all of his mental powers, Professor Xavier is able to control her and bring back the normal personality of Jean Grey. However, when the Dark Phoenix destroyed the planet, a multi-planetary commission of alien leaders determined that Jean Grey had to pay for the alien deaths, so they capture her. The X-Men fight valiantly, but in the end, knowing that her evil personality could return at any moment, Jean decides to sacrifice herself, throwing herself in front of a laser and dying in the arms of Cyclops, her soul mate.

That was how the story appeared in the comics, but that was not how Claremont and Byrne *wanted* the story to end. In their original version of the story, the X-Men try to protect Jean, but they fail, and then the alien forces use a device to eliminate her powers. For the next year or so, the readers would experience what it would be like to go from being one of the most powerful beings in the universe to being a normal human. Ultimately, Magneto would tempt Jean with a return of her powers, which would be the centerpiece of the next big X-Men story line.

That was the plan, but then editor in chief Jim Shooter stepped into the mix. Shooter felt that if she "only" had her powers taken away from her, that would not be a fair price to pay for murdering the planet of aliens. He felt that for such an act, she had to die, so he forced Claremont and Byrne to rewrite the story line.

Of course, this being comic books, a few years later, based on the idea of a comic book fan named Kurt Busiek (who later became a popular comic book writer in his own right), Marvel brought Jean Grey back to life, using the argument that the Phoenix was really a cosmic force that traded places with Jean Grey, so that it could experience life as a human, and Jean Grey was such an influence upon the cosmic being, that, though she was only a copy of Jean Grey, she was still willing to sacrifice herself for the greater good (their original version

© Marvel Comics

was later reprinted in a one-shot called *Phoenix: The Untold Story*).

ONE OF THE more enduring legacies of Chris Claremont's tenure as writer of *Uncanny X-Men* was the work he did with the character of Magneto. As created, Magneto was your typical bad guy, willing to destroy the whole world in a fit of pique. Claremont turned him into a tortured soul, a Jewish survivor of the Holocaust who feared that the same would happen to mutants, and he would not let that happen. Of course, in a strange twist, Marvel at one point decided to essentially do a reverse of what they did with the Thing and take *away* Magneto's Jewish heritage.

As with the Thing, Marvel was loathe to actually come out and state that Magneto was Jewish, because they did not like to address religion in their books. But during Claremont's time writing *X-Men*, it could not have been clearer if there were neon signs pointing at Magneto blinking the phrase "He is Jewish."

Over the years, Magneto discussed his time in Auschwitz, and everything he described there was consistent with being part of the Sonderkommando, the Jewish prisoners who, horrifically, were forced to do the dirty work of the Nazis in the death camps, like carting the dead bodies to be burned. Only Jews were in the Sonderkommando, but even so, in *X-Men Unlimited #2*, Marvel decided to turn its back on those years and specifically gave Magneto's origin as a Gypsy of Sinte descent named Erik Lensherr.

The decision came from editorial, and whatever the motivation was at the time, it has not been discussed, although it was likely

for the same reason that Stan Lee preferred not to discuss religion in the comics—why court controversy if you can avoid it? Ultimately, the "incontrovertible" evidence proving Magneto's history in *X-Men Unlimited* was, well, debunked—explained away as an excessively elaborate fraud by Magneto in 1997's *X-Men* #72. So while he has yet to be positively identified as Jewish in the comics, it appears that Marvel has returned him to that state, and Sir Ian McKellen's performance as Magneto in the X-Men films appears to portray him as Jewish, as well.

IN THE EARLY 1990s, Marvel Comics was in the midst of a humongous sales boom, with some titles selling over a million copies. In 1991 Marvel launched a second X-Men title. The first issue of the book indeed sold an uncanny seven million copies! During this time period, there were a number of young, popular artists who were really driving the sales of the Marvel titles. On *X-Men*, the artist was Jim Lee. Like John Byrne before him, Jim Lee began plotting the book with Claremont. However, as time went on, Lee wanted to have more and more of an influence over the book's direction, and when there was a difference of opinion between the two, the editor of the book, Bob Harras, tended to side with Lee, since Lee was seen as more directly responsible for the book's skyrocketing sales.

So after the first three issues of the second X-Men title (the royalties on those three issues were perhaps a final parting gift), for the first time in seventeen years Chris Claremont was no longer the writer of *The X-Men*. Jim Lee was given full control of *X-Men* (and teamed with popular fellow artist, Whilce Portacio, on the other X-Men title, *Uncanny X-Men*). John Byrne was brought back as a scripter for the series, but he was given increasingly ridiculous deadlines (Lee and Portacio were slow to deliver their plots, so Byrne would have to script them extremely fast). Editor Bob Harras felt he needed to get someone else to replace Byrne. His choice was Scott Lobdell, a fairly new Marvel writer who had only written a few lower-level Marvel titles at that point. The amusing thing was exactly *how* Lobdell was chosen.

It literally came down to the fact that Harras needed someone to script the book right at that moment, and Lobdell happened to walk past his office door. He gave the books to Lobdell to script, and Lobdell was able to handle the nearly impossible deadline (of course, in the confusion, no one bothered to tell Byrne that he was no longer the scripter on the book, which probably would have been nice). Soon after Lobdell signed on to script the books, however, Lee and Portacio both left Marvel to help cofound Image Comics. So after driving away the man who wrote the title for seventeen years, in favor of Lee and Portacio, Marvel was left without a writer for its two biggest books eight months into the new series. So Lobdell went from being the scripter for *Uncanny X-Men* to being the full writer (Fabian Nicieza took over *X-Men*), where he would stay for the next five years or so, going from an almost accidental hire to being the writer of *Uncanny X-Men* during some of its highest-selling years. Not bad for a guy who was in the office that day to talk to a totally different Marvel editor.

9

MARVEL COMICS MISCELLANEA

As alluded to a number of times earlier, Marvel was in a particularly precarious position at the end of the 1950s, when it came to the distribution of its comics. In fact, when the Marvel superhero boom of the 1960s hit, Marvel comics were actually being distributed by DC Comics. No, really!

During the early 1950s, when Timely changed its name to Atlas Comics, Martin Goodman distributed the comics through his own distribution company. However, toward the end of the decade he decided he wanted to expand the Atlas line of comics, so he signed a deal with American News Company, one of the largest distributors in the country, and a virtual monopoly. Actually, forget the "virtual" part, because in 1956 the U.S. government ruled that American News Company was a monopoly. Suddenly, Atlas was without a distributor, and since Goodman alienated all of his wholesalers when he made the move to American News, he could not go back to self-distribution. Therefore, his only recourse (besides shutting the company down entirely) was to go to Independent News, the distribution company owned by DC Comics!

Independent News agreed to the deal, under the condition that Atlas not publish more than eight books a month. Atlas went to a bimonthly schedule for all its books, which allowed it to put out sixteen titles, and with a bit of finagling it was sometimes able to put out ten books in one month if it put out six in the next.

This was particularly difficult during the early 1960s, when Marvel's popularity was increasing and it had a number of characters who could carry their own title. Marvel's only recourse was to split books between characters, which is why it had so many anthologies at that time, like *Tales to Astonish* and *Tales of Suspense*.

Eventually, in 1968, Marvel negotiated a slightly better deal from Independent News, which was when a number of its heroes received their own solo titles, including *Captain America*, *The Incredible Hulk*, and *Iron Man*. That same year, Marvel was sold to a company that eventually became known as Cadence Industries. In 1969, Cadence bought its own distributor, so Marvel was then free to put out as many comics as it wanted.

ARTISTS BREAK INTO working in comics in a variety of different manners, some stranger than others. But few have made as strange of an entry into the comic field as John Romita, the legendary comic book artist who, as noted earlier, was Steve Ditko's replacement on *Amazing Spider-Man* and for many years Marvel's art director. Romita received his big break by pretending to be someone else!

The story began in 1947, when Romita graduated from the School of Industrial Art, and after doing one story for Eastern Color Press's *Famous Funnies*, found himself without any work in comics. In 1949 he was making thirty dollars a week working in New York City for Forbes Lithograph, when he ran into a friend from art school named Lester Zakarin, who offered him the break he needed. Zakarin would pay Romita twenty dollars a page (almost as much as Romita was making in a week!) if Romita was willing to pencil a comic story for him and allow Zakarin to claim that it was his own artwork. Zakarin was an inker but could not pencil very well. Zakarin would ink Romita's pencils and submit the work as his own. The assignments were mostly for Stan Lee at Timely Comics.

One problem that arose was that Lee would often ask for corrections on the artwork from the penciller, and Zakarin could not make the corrections himself. The pair solved the problem by Romita going into the city with Zakarin and waiting at the New York Public Library, which was near Timely's offices. Zakarin would tell Lee that he could not draw in front of people—he needed complete silence to work. He would then say he was going to the apartment of a friend and would bring back the corrections later, but he would really go to the library. Romita would do the corrections there, and Zakarin would bring them back to Lee.

Eventually, Romita went to visit Lee's offices and told his secretary that while Lee did not know him, he had been working for him for over a year, and that he was the one actually drawing Zakarin's artwork. The secretary went to see Lee and returned with Romita's first assignment as John Romita. Of course, the kicker is that they assumed Romita was penciling and inking the comic, and Romita had never inked a comic before, but he was not about to risk losing the job, so he inked himself, for the first time ever. And he has never stopped working in comics for the past fifty years. Romita's son, also John, even became a Marvel artist and just recently celebrated thirty years of working at Marvel.

STEVE DITKO'S DISTASTE for Marvel (elaborated on pages 108–9) is well known. Even though he eventually did go back to working for Marvel in the late 1970s after Charlton, his preferred comic book employer, ceased to be a viable working choice, for a man who worked for Marvel well into the 1990s (when he more or less retired from regular comic book work), his displeasure with his past works for Marvel is so dramatic that he apparently even takes it out on his old work itself!

Up until the 1980s, original comic art was not returned to the artists. It was considered property of the comic companies, and, at

DC at least, old original artwork was eventually shredded (although certainly a number of pages "found" their way into the personal collections of DC staffers). During the 1980s, Marvel was in a dispute with artists over whether it owned the original work or was just paying for the production of the art, with the final ownership of the artwork belonging to the artists. Marvel eventually relented, under the following condition: it would give the artists back the art, but it would be as a *gift* out of Marvel's generosity. Marvel still believes that it owns the work fair and square but magnanimously allows the artists to have it. Ditko disagreed with this position vehemently and would not acknowledge the returned art.

This artwork, particularly when it features famous Marvel superhero characters, can easily sell for hundreds of dollars (and the really popular stuff for thousands) if the artist is famous like Ditko or Jack Kirby. However, when comic historian Greg Theakston visited Ditko a number of years ago, he noticed that the cutting board (which is exactly what it sounds like—a board on which you cut things) Ditko was using was an original cover from the 1950s! When Theakston expressed shock, Ditko told him to move a nearby curtain—behind it was a stack of original art almost two feet tall. Ditko wanted nothing to do with this old work and was in fact using it for cutting boards! When Steve Ditko takes a position, he takes it seriously.

IN THE EARLY 1970s, the toy company Mego began to produce a line of action figures, licensing superheroes from both Marvel and DC, including Spider-Man, Superman, Batman, and Captain America. The title of the line was World's Greatest Super-Heroes. Mego decided to apply for a trademark (and was granted one) for the term *super-hero*. DC and Marvel took issue with this and threatened legal action, which Mego avoided by giving up its rights to the term (some stories say it sold any rights it had for the nominal fee of one dollar).

DC and Marvel then decided to register the trademark themselves. It was granted in 1981, and just recently DC and Marvel filed renewal papers for the trademark. The idea of two companies sharing a trademark is uncommon but not that out of the ordinary. The theory behind the trademark is that when someone thinks of the word *super-hero*, they will almost certainly think of either a DC or a Marvel property, and if a comic book or a toy product comes out with the term *super-hero* on it, consumers will presume it is a DC or a Marvel product.

Marvel and DC have already kept one comic book creator from using the term *super-hero* in the title of his comic book (even though

it was spelled differently). They sent Dan Taylor, creator of the comic book *Super Hero Happy Hour* for the comic company Geek-Punk, a cease and desist letter.

© GeekPunk, Inc., image courtesy of Dan Taylor

While Taylor retitled the book *Hero Happy Hour* to avoid litigation, it would be interesting to see whether the trademark would hold up if anyone were to actually litigate the matter with Marvel and DC.

IN *FANTASTIC FOUR* #52, published in 1966, Stan Lee and Jack Kirby introduced the Black Panther, the first black superhero. T'Challa is the chief of the Panther tribe and also the ruler of the fictional African country Wakanda. His ceremonial title is the Black Panther. He wears an all-black costume with a panther mask and is a skilled fighter and one of the smartest men on planet Earth.

In 1968 T'Challa left Wakanda for a time to become a member of the superhero team the Avengers and to live in the United States under an assumed name to see what living as a typical American would be like. Eventually, he left the Avengers to return to rule his kingdom.

The Black Panther debuted in early 1966. In October of the same year, Huey P. Newton and Bobby Seale formed the Black Panther Party in Oakland, California. The group, which was initially designed to protect African American neighborhoods from police brutality, radicalized as time went on, as Newton and Seale's vision of "Power to the People!" split with other party members' view that the group should be about "Black Power!"

While this was going on, the Marvel comic book character continued to appear in the pages of *The Avengers*, but when he left the book in the early 1970s, Roy Thomas felt it would be prudent for Marvel to change T'Challa's name to something other than Black Panther. In *Fantastic Four* #119, the Thing and the Human Torch get caught up in an international problem when T'Challa, who is in pursuit of some bad guys, gets arrested in Rudyarda, a stand-in for South Africa. When Ben and Johnny free T'Challa, they are unprepared to hear him exclaim, as he knocks out a pair of guards, "You have done enough, Torch. Do not seek to do all of my fighting for me. Some things, after all, are best left to—the Black Leopard!"

When the Thing questions the name change, T'Challa explains that he plans on someday returning to the United States, and when he does, he knows that Black Panther has political connotations, and while "I neither condemn nor condone those who have taken up the name—but T'Challa is a law to himself. Hence, the new name—a minor point, at best, since the panther *is* a leopard."

© Marvel Comics

The name change did not last that long, and by the next time T'Challa showed up in a comic he was being called the Black Panther again. It probably had something to do with the Black Panther Party really coming apart a bit during the early 1970s. If it had remained more of a cohesive, active unit, it is likely that Marvel would have continued to distance itself from it, but by the early 1970s it was more or less nonexistent, as far as a serious radical party goes. The Black Panther, meanwhile, has had a few series since then, including a current ongoing title, in which he has taken the X-Man Storm as his wife and the new queen of Wakanda.

Luke Cage, Hero for Hire was a Marvel comic that was one of the first books to star an African American superhero. Carl Lucas was thrown into prison as a young man for a crime he did not commit.

© Marvel Comics

He agreed to participate in some experiments in exchange for his parole. The experiments were nominally designed to help cure illnesses but instead resulted in Lucas gaining skin that was bulletproof and becoming a great deal stronger. After being cheated out of his parole, Lucas decided to escape from prison, and once on the outside, he took the name Luke Cage and made himself available as a superhero for hire (although he usually turned down payment when it came to that point).

After a while Marvel decided to help the book's sales by giving Lucas an official superhero name, Power Man. This still did not help sales that much, so Marvel decided to team him up with a similarly low-selling title, the kung fu comic *Iron Fist*. *Power Man and Iron Fist* was a success, lasting six years.

Luke Cage made an impact at Marvel, being its first comic starring an African American hero, but it also had an impact in an area outside of comics, namely in the world of acting.

Aspiring actor Nicolas Coppola was concerned that wherever he went there were sneers and cries of nepotism because of his famous last name, courtesy of his uncle, the legendary film director Francis Ford Coppola. So the young Coppola decided to pick a stage name. He had always been a big fan of superheroes, ever since he learned how to read by reading comics, so he ended up taking the last name Cage, perhaps seeing something of himself in the streetwise hero. In later years, Cage would note that he also enjoyed the work of the avant-garde composer John Cage, and some people presume it was he whom Cage took his name from. But in recent years, Cage has made it clear that, while he enjoys the work of John Cage, it was Luke Cage that inspired his name.

From the Marvel Comics adapted film *Ghost Rider.*

Cage's interest in comics did not end there. He put together an extensive comic collection, which he sold (after he married Lisa Marie Presley) for 1.6 million dollars. In addition, his son with his current wife, Alice Kim, is named Kal-El, after Superman's Kryptonian name. Cage even played a superhero recently in the film version of *Ghost Rider.*

As noted earlier (on pages 140–41), Steve Englehart was a popular writer for Marvel who was not one to shy from controversial topics, including the story line he did for *Doctor Strange* during the early 1970s, which got so touchy that he felt it necessary to fake a letter from a minister to support himself!

Doctor Strange was created by Stan Lee and Steve Ditko, and it tells the story of a rich and powerful surgeon named Stephen Strange who has a callous disregard for humanity. When a car accident causes his hands to shake too much to do surgery anymore, Strange searches for a hermit known as the Ancient One who could cure him. When he finds him, the Ancient One refuses to cure him but offers him an apprenticeship in the mystic arts. Strange refuses, but after discovering that the Ancient One's current apprentice, Baron Mordo, is trying to kill the Ancient One, Strange's humanity finally returns. He takes the apprenticeship so that he can learn enough magic to stop Mordo. A new man, Strange becomes the most powerful magician in the world, the Sorcerer Supreme, as it were, and dedicates his life to helping humanity.

Englehart began work on the character in 1973, with artist Frank Brunner, in an epic story in which Doctor Strange follows around a being called Sise-Neg (*genesis* backward) who turns out to be God, and Strange is there when God creates the universe. When the issue was released, Stan Lee was frantic. Marvel needed to print a retraction to say the character was not God, just a god. Englehart and Brunner felt this would ruin the story, so they came up with a plan. Englehart happened to be traveling through Texas for one reason or another (a comic convention perhaps), so they created a fictional person, a Rev. Billingsley in Texas, who wrote a letter saying that a young boy in his parish had given him the comic and the reverend felt it was the best comic he ever read!

Marvel then told Englehart that he did not have to print the retraction. Instead, it was going to print the letter in the letters column as proof that the story was not offensive!

NOT ONLY DID Luke Cage's name have an effect on Nicolas Cage, but his superhero name, Power Man, led to a bit of an amusing spat between Marvel and DC over the word *power*.

In 1964 Marvel introduced a new member of the Avengers, Wonder Man. He turned out to be a bad guy in disguise, but in the end he became a good guy, sacrificing his life to save the Avengers. Apparently, though, DC was miffed that Marvel was using the word *wonder*, because it felt that it took away from its character Wonder Woman. Wonder Man dies in the issue in question, so it was not a pressing matter, but Marvel agreed anyway not to have a character named Wonder Man.

A decade later, Marvel gave Luke Cage his new superhero name, Power Man. A year later, though, former Marvel employee Gerry Conway introduced a new member of the DC's All Star Super Squad—Power Girl, Superman's cousin.

Whether DC actually gave Marvel problems or not, the key was that Jim Shooter *believed* that DC had given Marvel a problem over the use of the word *wonder,* and then a year after Marvel introduced Power Man, DC introduces Power Girl? That was certainly cause for irritation.

So Shooter quickly moved for Wonder Man to come back from the dead. He did so in *The Avengers* #151 and #152, which came out later in the same year as Power Girl's debut. An interesting situation happened in *The Avengers* #151. Because of delays over the script (Steve Englehart had left the title but still owed a script for his last issue), Gerry Conway (who had come back to Marvel) ended up scripting part of *The Avengers* #151 for Shooter, so Conway ended up both introducing Power Girl, which caused the problem, *and* writing Marvel's retort to Power Girl's introduction—so he was essentially responding to himself!

Wonder Man ended up becoming a popular Marvel character and even had his own title for a few years in the 1990s. Power Girl, though, has also been a popular DC character, and it was recently announced that she too would be getting her own ongoing title.

As mentioned (on pages 127–28), Marvel has been very protective of its trademarks over the years, and that includes being on constant lookout for names that might be used that are similar to notable Marvel characters. This was the case when Marvel raced to come up with a Spider-Woman character so as to register a trademark of the name before another company used it.

The cartoon studio Filmation Associates had a cartoon show starring Tarzan in the mid-1970s. It found that the show was even more popular when it was combined with Batman the next season to form *The Batman / Tarzan Adventure Hour.* Seeing that this arrangement was working, Filmation's next move was to expand the show to include five other superhero characters, this time all-new characters (so Filmation would not have to pay licensing fees, like they had to for Batman). Well, one of those new characters was to be called Spider-Woman.

When news of this came down the grapevine, Marvel knew it had to respond quickly, for fear that Filmation would have something published first. So writer Ar-chie Goodwin had to come up with a Spider-Woman character and concept for Marvel in a very short period of time. With the help of artists Sal Buscema and Jim Mooney, Marvel rushed production of *Marvel Spotlight* #32, starring Spider-Woman.

The filing for trademark protection was almost instantaneous. The comic was released in very late 1976, and Marvel was awarded trademark protection in early 1977. Hanna-Barbera Filmation ended up changing its character's name to Webwoman.

In his rush to get a product out there, Archie Goodwin actually ended up using Len Wein's initial origin story for Wolverine (as noted on pages 151–52). In her first appearance, Spider-Woman is an actual spider evolved by the High Evolutionary into a Spider-Woman, just like Len Wein had planned for Wolverine. In fact, note that the last time the *X-Men* comics mentions the origin is in 1976, right before the creation of Spider-Woman! It is more

likely that Chris Claremont just chose to use a different origin of his own volition, but it is not outside the realm of possibility that he was told that the mutated-wolverine origin was off-limits after it was used for Spider-Woman.

Afterward, when Marvel had time to think the character out, Marv Wolfman was assigned to write Spider-Woman's ongoing series, and the first thing he did? Get rid of the mutated-spider origin.

SPEAKING OF PICKING up good names, in 1964 Stan Lee grabbed a great name that had gone unprotected while a rival company was out of business, when he launched *Daredevil* #1, using the same name of the popular Lev Gleason Publishing hero of the 1940s. Daredevil was an interesting character for Marvel, and his origins had an even more interesting source.

Daredevil followed in Stan Lee's formula of heroes with problems. The titular hero was Matt Murdock, a successful lawyer who was blinded as a child when he pushed an old man out of the way of a truck carrying radioactive waste. The waste hit Matt in the face, blinding him but also secretly giving him a sort of radar sense that allows him to "see" people, in some way, better than other people can because all of his other senses were enhanced.

Stan Lee has spoken on the topic of the origin of Daredevil, and he claims that the idea was his. Still, there are situations in the life of artist and cocreator Bill Everett that seem to suggest that Lee may be mistaken. Bill Everett's daughter, Wendy, is legally blind, and she recalls that she and her father discussed the idea of a blind superhero, partially based on the fact that her other senses were more highly attuned due to the loss of her sight, which would seem to translate well to a superpower.

So while Lee feels that he came up with the idea on his own, when the other cocreator of a blind superhero has a blind daughter, whether she remembers her father creating the character or not (which, in this instance, she does), it seems to suggest that the odds are that Everett had more to do with the blind part of Daredevil than Lee believes.

STAN LEE OCCASIONALLY finds himself in a position where his often unreliable memory gets him into a bit of trouble, which was the case when he tried to out a comic character from the 1960s.

Lee was being interviewed in 2002 by a conservative group, the Traditional Values Coalition, discussing a recent Marvel comic miniseries that starred a Marvel Western character from the 1950s and '60s, Rawhide Kid, in which it was revealed that said character was gay. The issue caused a bit of an uproar, and while being interviewed, Lee attempted to downplay the significance of the character being gay. In fact, said Lee, it is not even that surprising, as Lee had written gay characters into some of his comics in the past. The claim seemed a bit dubious, so the interviewer asked him to name one, and Lee decided to name Percival "Percy" Pinkerton, a member of Sgt. Fury's Howling Commandos.

© Marvel Comics

Pinkerton's first appearance from *Sgt. Fury* #8, with art by Dick Ayers.

This decision came as a surprise to readers of that series, as Lee had always written the character, who was based on the British actor David Niven, as a bit of a playboy—very much interested in women. Another voice of dissent was artist Dick Ayers, who worked on the series with Lee after Jack Kirby left. He said that this current view of Percy Pinkerton bore no resemblance to how Lee wrote the character at the time—and Ayers should know, since he worked with Lee on the character.

It appears that Lee was basing his sudden choice on the facts that he had written the British character to be a bit of a fop and that his name has the word *pink* in it. Not much to go on, but it had been forty years since Lee had written for the character. Ultimately, Lee admitted that, yes, he was just confused and had misremembered the character.

* * *

WHILE BOTH DC and Marvel had their share of popular successes with licensed comics, when Marvel first began considering them in 1970, it was extremely wary. In fact, Stan Lee originally turned down the chance to produce Conan the Barbarian comic books!

Roy Thomas was a huge fan of the classic Robert E. Howard pulp series about the mighty barbarian, Conan, who is a Cimmerian warrior who slowly worked his way up from his life as a thief until he was eventually king. Howard's stories were widely influential in the world of fantasy, and Thomas was not the only one at Marvel who was pushing for a Conan series—artist Gil Kane had wanted to do one for years.

However, Stan Lee did not think that publisher Martin Goodman would go for paying the licensing fee. Thomas wrote a detailed memo explaining to Goodman why it made sense to not just do a sword-and-sorcery book but to specifically license one of the famous sword-and-sorcery characters, because that was what the fans were writing in for and specifically asking about. They weren't saying, "Give us fantasy comics," but "Give us Conan comics!"

Ultimately, Thomas's memo was so persuasive that Goodman opened up a small licensing budget and left it to Lee to determine which book they would go after licensing. Lee decided not to pursue Conan; instead he authorized Thomas to try to license author Lin Carter's barbarian hero Thongor, only because Lee thought Thongor sounded like a more interesting name than Conan. Thomas contacted Carter, but there was an impasse: Carter was looking for more than the $150 licensing fee Thomas was authorized to spend. When Carter stalled, Thomas made an executive decision and decided to contact the representatives for Conan.

When Thomas sealed the deal, he had a problem getting an artist, because the two artists who would most love doing a Conan comic, Gil Kane and John Buscema, were too expensive for the extremely small budget Goodman gave the new title. Since he was on a budget, Thomas had to use a cheap artist, but lucky for him that cheap artist was Barry Windsor-Smith, a young penciller who would soon become a major comic book star due to his detailed and striking action work on *Conan the Barbarian*.

The book started slow, saleswise, but sales soon kicked in, and before too long, Marvel was publishing multiple Conan comic books, as well as a black-and-white magazine starring Conan. Suddenly, John Buscema and Gil Kane were affordable for the comic.

© Marvel Comics

YOU WOULD NOT think that lightning would strike twice, but in a way that is what happened later in the decade when Stan Lee turned down the opportunity to do a *Star Wars* comic book!

In 1976 Roy Thomas received a visit at his apartment from Charley Lippincott, who was in charge of merchandising and publicity for *Star Wars*, and he told Thomas that George Lucas wanted Marvel to adapt *Star Wars* into a comic book form to be released before the movie to drum up interest in the film. He admired Thomas's work as an adapter for the Howard comic titles (which, by this time, numbered quite a few comics), and specifically asked for him to do the adaptation.

Thomas, of course, appreciated the flattery, but told him that he had not been editor in chief of Marvel in a few years, so he had better talk to Stan Lee. Lippincott then told him that he had, that and Lee had turned him down flat. Now, Thomas was wondering what they expected from him—and they had their answer. They asked to show him a series of paintings detailing the story of *Star Wars*, and he acquiesced. By the middle of the presentation, Thomas was hooked. He was willing to talk Lee into doing the adaptation, which was simpler than Thomas thought, perhaps mostly because adapting a film before it is released is basically doing advertisement for the film—so it does not cost much in terms of licensing fees.

The adaptation turned out to be helpful for the film but hugely beneficial for Marvel (although Thomas left fairly early on, because the *Star Wars* people were a bit too hands-on with their comments).

In the years since, Jim Shooter, Marvel editor in chief at the time, has said that Marvel was in rough shape in the late 1970s, and the massive sales success of *Star Wars* helped save the company. So it seems that all's well that ends well—just so long as you don't take your first no from Stan Lee as the final answer.

SINCE HE STARTED inking *Conan* with issue #26 in 1973, artist Ernesto "Ernie" Chan has inked more pages of *Conan* artwork than any other artist in comic book history. However, shockingly, for years the popular artist had to go under a different name—all because of a typographical error!

Born in the Philippines in 1940, Chan worked in the Philippines comic industry, along such great Filipino artists as Alfredo Alcala, Tony DeZuniga, Nestor Redondo, Danny Bulandi, and Romeo Tanghal. DeZuniga was one of the first Filipino artists to hit it big in America, so Chan came to the United States to apprentice with him in the very early 1970s. Eventually Chan got work at DC

Comics and then at Marvel, where he began his long tenure as inker for *Conan*.

While working on covers at DC, though, Chan had an interesting credit—his work was signed Ernie Chua. The problem was that there was a typographical error on Chan's birth certificate, so when he immigrated to the United States, that is the name that was on his immigration papers, and therefore on his other legal documents, including all his tax papers. When he became a U.S. citizen, he was able to go back to his actual name and began being credited correctly.

Years later, Chan was asked why the immigration officials weren't willing to fix the simple error, and he gave a rather scary answer. The official told him the erroneous name would be better for him, because "there are too many Chans in the United States."

ANOTHER INTERESTING TIE-IN with another medium took place in the late 1970s, when Casablanca Records contacted Marvel about a new comic book idea. Casablanca Records was founded by Neil Bogart, and it was at the forefront of the disco revolution, with, among others, its biggest star, Donna Summer. While Casablanca was mostly known for its disco records, it was also the record company of the rock band Kiss.

In any event, in the late 1970s, Casablanca approached Marvel about doing a comic book series about a singer. Marvel would create the series about the singer, and then Casablanca would provide a singer who matched that description, and it would be a back-and-forth joint publicity effort. The comics would promote her records, and the records would promote the comic book, and there was also going to be a film tie-in. It was a fine idea, but it all fell apart after the initial development because Casablanca just couldn't determine what it wanted exactly from writer Tom De-Falco, besides something along the lines of a character named the

Disco Queen. The project ultimately ended up in developmental limbo.

It stayed in limbo until almost two years later, when the project resurfaced, this time as a film starring Bo Derek (the record tie-in might have still been in play, but I do not believe so), which would be called *Dazzler*. So the features of the character (which were originally those of an African American woman) were changed to be like Bo Derek, and the character made her debut in an issue of *Uncanny X-Men*.

© Marvel Comics

The film never came to be, but *Dazzler* has been a mainstay in the Marvel Universe ever since.

WHILE BO DEREK might have enjoyed seeing being immortalized in a comic book, one performer who had a major problem with it was singer Amy Grant.

In 1986 Amy Grant released *The Collection*, a greatest-hits package of her work to that point, which became an extremely popular album (going platinum at least once).

In early 1990, *Doctor Strange: Sorcerer Supreme* #15 came out. It was the second part of a five-part story that involved Marie Laveau, based on a real-life American woman who practiced voodoo in New Orleans in the nineteenth century. On the cover, artist Jackson Guice depicted the character named Morgana Blessing with a look familiar to Amy Grant fans—the image of Grant as it appeared on the cover of *The Collection*.

Soon after the issue came to their attention, Amy Grant's management team, Mike Blanton and Dan Harrell, quickly filed a complaint

© Mark Tucker

against Marvel Comics. Here is where it gets tricky. They were not, as many folks think, suing over copyright infringement. First off, the

copyright for the photo belonged to photographer Mark Tucker (an accomplished Nashville commercial photographer, whose work has graced a number of records), so that wouldn't work.

No, the complaint, filed by Blanton and Harrell in federal court in Tennessee, was related more to the fear that it would appear that Grant was authorizing the use of her likeness and was therefore condoning the comic book, which would affect her standing in the Christian music community. Reading from the complaint: "Many fans of Christian music consider interest in witchcraft and the occult to be antithetical to their Christian beliefs and to the message of Christian music in general. Therefore, an association of Amy Grant or her likeness [with Doctor Strange] . . . is likely to cause irreparable injury to Grant's reputation and good will."

A U.S. district court sealed an out-of-court settlement between Grant and Marvel in early 1991, with a consent decree that Marvel did not admit to any liability or wrongdoing.

The issue may or may not have been asked to be pulled from stores, but since it was a monthly book, such an order really doesn't have much of an effect. An order to remove is not that effective when the item is a periodical, since the issue is usually sold out by the time it is ordered to be removed, and in fact sometimes the next issue has already come out!

GHOST RIDER, WHICH was made into a film recently starring Nicolas Cage, is the tale of a motorcycle stunt rider named Johnny Blaze who sold his soul to Satan to save someone he loves, which resulted in Blaze becoming bonded to a demon named Zarathos. When using his powers, Blaze's flesh is consumed by hellfire, causing him to have a flaming skull. He also rides a motorcycle made out of flames. With all this talk of demons, you might think that there might be some religious controversy surrounding *Ghost Rider,* and if so, you would be correct.

When the creator of *Ghost Rider,* Gary Friedrich, left the book, writer Tony Isabella took over the title.

Soon into his run, Isabella decided to have the book break away from Friedrich's style (presumably thinking, "He did it so well, let's try something different"), and Isabella made Ghost Rider into a bit more of a superhero. At the same time, he also attempted to examine some themes of redemption with the character.

One of the first things Isabella did (using a suggestion by writer Steve Gerber, to whom Isabella had told his plans for the book) was to introduce, as a supporting character, none other than Jesus Christ. The idea being that since Ghost Rider had a deal with Satan, wouldn't God want to get involved? Thus we saw the introduction of the Friend, a sage traveler with long hair and a beard who would assist Ghost Rider in redeeming himself.

The story line continued for two years. However, when it came down to the conclusion, the book's editor, Jim Shooter, took issue with the story line, as he disagreed with the idea of having Jesus in the book.

Therefore, for *Ghost Rider* #19, Shooter rewrote the issue and had some of the art partially redrawn. The new story revealed that the Friend was actually a demonic illusion meant to trick Ghost Rider. Shooter felt this was less offensive than Jesus Christ actually appearing in a comic book. Isabella, expectedly, disagreed and quit the book.

A little while later, writer Roger Stern took over the book and made another change to the story of Ghost Rider in the name of being inoffensive to the religious. Now, rather than it being Satan who Johnny Blaze was involved with, it was the fictional Marvel demon Mephisto (who first appeared as a nemesis of the Silver Surfer). Stern thought it made more sense for it to be an established Marvel character behind Ghost Rider's origin and, at the same time, that it would be less offensive to religious readers who believe in Satan.

It's interesting to see how religiously sensitive Marvel is over what is essentially a demon riding a motorcycle! I doubt the extremely religious would be pleased with the concept no matter what.

JIM STARLIN'S RUN as writer-artist of *Warlock* was one of the most acclaimed comic book runs of the 1970s. Starlin masterfully worked into the story line a gigantic space opera involving a genetically engineered human named Adam Warlock, a green female assassin named Gamora, and a foul-mouthed troll named Pip, issues with organized religion and the difficulties that arise in personal-identity conflicts (personified in a hero fighting against his evil self from the future).

While the series was critically acclaimed, it did not sell that well, and Starlin ultimately had to resolve all of his story lines in the pages of other comic book titles. He did write one last issue of *Warlock* in the late 1970s, which was drawn by artist Alan Weiss and designed as an inventory story in case Marvel ever had use for it (during the 1980s Marvel actually started a series that published the best of these inventory stories, called *Marvel Fanfare*). A strange problem quickly arose, though, when the artwork for the issue disappeared. The reason for the disappearance was even stranger. It had been left in the backseat of a cab!

Weiss had just flown into New York, and some folks from Marvel met him at the airport to help him carry his belongings, as he was going to move in with another Marvel artist, Al Milgrom.

When he arrived, one of the people there (Weiss specifically refuses to say who, but it is worth noting that when he tells the story he names everyone who was there except the fellow whose apartment he was going to share) helped him carry his bags, and this person picked up a box containing the pencils for *Warlock* #16. When they arrived at the apartment, the box was missing—presumably circulating in a cab somewhere in the New York metropolitan area!

Interestingly enough, copies were apparently made of the issue, so during the early 1990s there were plans to redo the issue for *Marvel Fanfare*, but then *Marvel Fanfare* was canceled. Then later on in the 1990s, Marvel planned to feature the story as a special issue of Warlock's current book (Starlin had relaunched the character's title in 1992), but then *that* book was canceled before they had a chance.

The fates, it seems, do not want *Warlock* #16 to ever see print.

IF IT WAS Milgrom who lost the art, he made an even bigger mistake some years later—a mistake so big that he lost his job over it!

At the turn of the twenty-first century, Milgrom was working on the Marvel staff as an inker. He would ink some books and troubleshoot for other books that needed help with deadlines. At the time, the editor in chief at Marvel was Bob Harras. Harras was fired in August 2000 and replaced with Marvel's current editor in chief, Joe Quesada.

Milgrom was one of three inkers on a one-shot comic called *Universe X: Spidey* (*Universe X* was part of a trilogy of alternate-future comics, after the success of a similar concept called *Kingdom Come* that Alex Ross had cocreated for DC Comics with Mark Waid), inking the pencils of Jackson Guice (the artist from the Amy Grant incident on pages 181–82). At one point in the story, Al Milgrom snuck into the background of a panel, along the spines of books on a bookshelf: "Harras, ha ha, he's gone! Good riddance to bad rubbish. He was a nasty SOB."

The panel was caught before the book went to print, but, apparently due a communication error in the production department, the book was printed with the panel intact. Marvel then pulped the entire print run and reprinted the book with the panel edited. At the time, the higher-ups at Marvel wanted to terminate Milgrom and never have him work for Marvel again.

Ultimately, Quesada managed to get them to allow Milgrom to continue to work at Marvel on a freelance basis, although his staff position was taken away. Also, part of his payments would be deducted to pay for the cost of pulping and reprinting the comic (a sizable amount of money, well over twenty thousand dollars). Jim Starlin quickly arranged for Milgrom to work on a number of projects with him. Nowadays, though, Milgrom is working as an inker mostly for Archie Comics.

An interesting (and relatively believable) conspiracy theory that the issue was printed even after the mistake was caught because the pulping of the book would be "just cause" to terminate Milgrom without having to pay him severance. This seems unlikely, as it is doubtful that the severance would be any cheaper than the cost of pulping the book, not to mention the time and effort to do the pulping and to supervise the new printing.

Amusingly enough, when the issue was reprinted as part of the *Universe X* collection a year or so later, the same mistake was repeated—so the trade paperback was printed with the insult still there!

MARK GRUENWALD WAS a beloved editor and writer at Marvel Comics for many years. Gruenwald was heavily involved in comic book fandom prior to being hired at Marvel in 1978, where he quickly rose in the ranks to becoming a full editor. He was a fixture of Marvel until his death in 1996, and it is only fitting that a piece of him lived on at the company after his death.

Despite a remarkable eight-year run as the writer of *Captain America*, the work that Gruenwald was most proud of at Marvel was *Squadron Supreme*. Created by Roy Thomas as a joke between Thomas, then writer of *The Avengers*, and Denny O'Neil, then writer of DC's *Justice League*, the Squadron was made up of analogues to DC's Justice League. Hyperion was Superman, Nighthawk was Batman, Power Princess was Wonder Woman, etc. The Squadron Supreme lived on an alternate Earth. In 1985 Gruenwald did a twelve-issue series detailing what happened when the Squadron Supreme decided to use their powers to fix our Earth, by taking it over themselves. It was a brilliant look at a realistic demonstration of what superheroes could do in the "real" world and whether it was something that would be at all beneficial for society. A benevolent tyranny is still tyranny. The series is well remembered as one of the first "serious" comics, and Alan Moore's classic series *Watchmen*, which began the next year, is similar in scope.

When Gruenwald died of a heart attack in 1996, his will asked that he be cremated and that his ashes be mixed with the ink used to print a comic book by Marvel. The Marvel editor in chief at the time, Bob Harras, along with Mark's widow, Catherine, decided to choose the first printing of the first trade paperback compilation of *Squadron Supreme*.

Mark Gruenwald was part of Marvel for almost two decades—now he will be part of Marvel Comics forever.

© Marvel Comics, image courtesy of Kelson Vibber and Matt Hunter

Part Three

OTHER COMIC BOOK COMPANIES

While Marvel and DC may snag the lion's share of the comic book market, they are far from the only comic book companies out there. The following are probably the five most notable "other" companies out there: Image, Dark Horse, Archie, Fantagraphics, and Top Shelf.

Image Comics is the brainchild of a number of popular Marvel artists who decided in the early 1990s that they were bigger than the comics they were doing at Marvel and that their fans would follow them wherever they went. So why not produce their own titles, with the freedom to do whatever they want and at a higher percentage of the income? The founding members of Image were Todd McFarlane, Jim Lee, Rob Liefeld, Erik Larsen, Marc Silvestri, Jim Valentino, and Whilce Portacio. The group was designed so that the seven men would each form an autonomous studio, but under the banner of Image Comics (Portacio decided to work through Lee's studio, so there were only six original studios at Image). Since the formation of Image, Liefeld has left the group, and so has Jim Lee (Lee sold his studio to DC Comics). The company is still going strong, and is now one of the largest independent comic companies in the industry.

Mike Richardson started Dark Horse Comics in 1986, figuring it would be a nice side business to the chain of comic book stores he owned in the Pacific Northwest. Over twenty years later, Dark Horse is the third-largest comic book company in the country. Richardson began by courting less-established artists that he felt did strong work, but when he saw that the company might actually be more than a side project, he began seeking more-popular artists, and in his best business move he began attempting to license film properties. Richardson broke into the licensing market in an ingenious manner: if he could not get a license outright, he would license whatever he could from the company, whether it be making a statute or an action figure or stationery. He formed valuable connections, and within a few years, Dark Horse had some of the most notable licenses in comics, including *Star Wars*, *Aliens*, and *Predator*.

In the early 1990s, Dark Horse formed a new company, Dark Horse Entertainment, which would attempt to make films based on Dark Horse comics. Their very first production was *The Mask*, starring Jim Carrey and Cameron Diaz (in her first film), and it was a smash hit.

Today Dark Horse does a mixture of licensed properties (*Star Wars*, *Buffy*, *Conan*) and acclaimed comics with a slight horror tint (*The Goon*, *Hellboy*, *Umbrella Academy*), while still being involved in film. Its second film based on the *Hellboy* comic book was released in 2008.

Archie Comics is one of the longest-running comic companies out there. It came into existence as MLJ Comics in 1939 but changed its name to Archie in 1946 after its breakout character, Archie Andrews, who first appeared in 1941 (see page 135). Archie is a seemingly average redheaded teen who has two lovely young ladies, Betty and Veronica, constantly fighting for his attention. His girl-hating best friend, Jughead, keeps him company; while Reggie Mantle is his rival at most everything in life, except for when Archie is at school, where the principal, Waldo Weatherbee, is the one making trouble for Archie.

Over the years, the Archie universe has expanded, with such notable characters as Sabrina the Teenage Witch and Josie and the Pussycats, both creations of the legendary artist Dan DeCarlo.

The wholesome nature of the Archie line of comics is attractive to other media, and Archie, Josie, and Sabrina have all had popular animated television series, while Sabrina also had a long-lasting live-action series. Josie and the Pussycats had a film a few years ago, and in the 1960s a group passing itself off as Archie's band, the Archies, even had a number one hit single with "Sugar, Sugar."

Perhaps the greatest innovation by Archie Comics was to design a strict house style for its artwork (since DeCarlo joined the company in the 1950s, his style has been the basic house style), which allows its comics from the 1960s, '70s, '80s, and '90s to look quite similar to the comics produced today. Therefore Archie Comics is able to run an extensive digest-reprint system, because it has decades of stories to choose from, all in the same basic style! *Archie* comic digests are often the only comics you can still buy at a supermarket checkout aisle.

In 1976 Gary Groth formed Fantagraphics Books with Mike Catron. Kim Thompson joined the next year, and ever since then Fantagraphics has been devoted to delivering some of the best and brightest independent comic books that the industry has to offer. The number of critically acclaimed artists who work through Fantagraphics is practically incalculable. Highlights of the roster include Chris Ware's *Acme Novelty Library*, which gave the world *Jimmy Corrigan, the Smartest Kid on Earth* (the first comic book to receive the Guardian First Book Award); Gilbert and Jaime Hernandez's *Love and Rockets*; Peter Bagge's *Hate*; and Daniel Clowes's *Ghost World*.

Fantagraphics also does extensive work reprinting classic comic strips, with its current series of *Peanuts* strips being a particularly big hit.

Top Shelf Productions is a veritable baby compared to these other companies. Formed in 1997 by Chris Staros and Brett Warnock, but in just eleven years it has amassed one of the greatest collections of talent in the industry, including Alex Robinson and Craig Thompson, but its most notable addition to the world of comics is that it's the only American comic company that you are going to see with comics by Alan Moore, as it snared him when he officially parted ways with DC/Wildstorm. It already had the rights to his classic *From Hell* series, but recently it published his controversial *Lost Girls* hardcover collection (a series of erotica, starring Dorothy from *The Wizard of Oz*, Wendy from *Peter Pan*, and Alice from *Alice's Adventures in Wonderland*), and will be publishing his future *League of Extraordinary Gentlemen* works.

On Alan Moore's name alone, the company begs to be paid attention to, but really so do most of the independent comic book companies out there, each of which seems to have at least one or two notable works. In addition, a number of distinguished comic book companies that have been out of business for years, like Fawcett, Quality, EC, Harvey, Fox, Lev Gleason, Dell, Gold Key, Charlton, and even most of the Disney comic titles are no longer published in the United States.

10

WALT DISNEY COMICS

Walt Disney comics first began appearing in newspaper comic strips in 1930 with a Mickey Mouse strip. In 1932 *Mickey Mouse* gained a partner when the strip was joined by the *Silly Symphonies* strip, which starred various Disney characters. In 1934 Donald Duck first appeared in the *Silly Symphonies* strip and soon took over the strip entirely. The Mickey Mouse strips were drawn by acclaimed comic artist Floyd Gottfredson for over forty years, while the Donald Duck strips were drawn by Al Taliaferro.

In 1940 Western Publishing purchased the rights to the Disney strips and began reprinting them, through a partnership with Dell Comics, in the pages of *Four Color Comics*. The reprint books were so popular that in 1940 they soon decided to start a brand-new title featuring original made-for-comic-books content, *Walt Disney's Comics and Stories*. It was in this series that Carl Barks began his legendary run on the Disney titles. *Walt Disney's Comics and Stories* became one of the most popular comics series of the 1950s, selling in the millions per month. In 1961 Western formed its own comic book company, Gold Key, which took over the Disney titles.

In 1947 Barks introduced a new character in a Christmas story in *Walt Disney's Comics and Stories* #178, "Christmas on Bear Mountain." The character, Scrooge McDuck, was a takeoff of Ebenezer Scrooge from the Charles Dickens Christmas classic *A Christmas Carol*. He was a hit with readers, and after a few more guest appearances in Donald Duck stories, Scrooge received his own title, *Uncle Scrooge*, in 1952. Along with *Walt Disney Comics and Stories*, they are the only Disney comic books that are still published in the United States.

While Disney comics are surprisingly not that popular in the United States, where it is difficult keeping even two Disney titles afloat, they are massively successful in the rest of the world, especially Europe. While sales in Europe have cooled off a bit in recent years, they still sell quite well in most countries—higher than the most successful comics in the United States (and considering the population differences between the United States and countries like, say, Denmark, it is quite impressive how well the books sell).

The most notable Disney comic book artist is the aforementioned Carl Barks, who was so popular among readers of the comics that he was given a name by fans back when Disney did not list credits in its comics. He was known worldwide as the Good Duck Artist and the Duck Man because his Donald Duck (and later, his Uncle Scrooge) stories were considered to be a step ahead of the rest, even the great artists like Tony Strobl and Paul Murry.

Nowadays, William Van Horn and Don Rosa are the two biggest names in Disney comics, although neither of them work for U.S. comic companies. They both work for European companies, but they work from the United States. Rosa is a devoted fan of Barks, and much of Rosa's work is a sort of tribute to Barks's comics. Rosa's work has developed a strong critical following, and he has gotten a great deal of award recognition for his *Uncle Scrooge* comics.

OF THE MANY things that change in a culture over the years, sense of humor is right up there with acceptable lengths of women's skirts and men's hair. Some jokes that were commonplace in 1932 are avoided now because they are racist, sexist, and/or xenophobic, which is certainly a change for the better. However, there are other jokes that were acceptable then and would be shocking now that are more a matter of being daring with characters that the audience is used to seeing portrayed as fairly bland. It is striking to note that while Disney would most likely never dream of doing anything edgy with Mickey Mouse in 2008, Walt Disney himself was willing to do so almost eighty years ago.

When the *Mickey Mouse* comic strip began in 1930, Disney wrote the strip along with penciling by Ub Iwerks (cocreator of Mickey Mouse) and inking by Win Smith. Iwerks left the strip soon after it began, and Smith took on both penciling and inking. Soon Disney became so busy with running his company that he did not have the time to write the comic, at which point Smith balked at the prospect of going from simply being the inker of the strip to being the inker, penciller, and writer—so he quit. Disney then went to a recent hire at the company, Floyd Gottfredson, to take over. Gottfredson had been hired as an animator and was told that the newspaper strip assignment would just be temporary—until they could find a permanent replacement for Smith. The "temporary" assignment lasted from 1930 until 1975, when Gottfredson retired.

Gottfredson's first story line was a continuation of an adventure Disney and Smith began, but in the fall of 1930 he was on his own. However, Disney managed to free up enough time to suggest a plot for Gottfredson, which he used in October of 1930, and it was a strange one.

Disney's idea was that Mickey would see his girlfriend, Minnie Mouse, with another guy, then Mickey would go home and kill himself! The joke being that every time Mickey tried to commit suicide, something would happen that would foul up the attempt. Like right before he shoots himself in the head with a shotgun, a cuckoo clock rings out, making Mickey realize it would be cuckoo to shoot himself in the face. In the next strip, he jumps off a bridge, but lands on a boat below! The captain thinks he is a stowaway, but Mickey pleads with him not to throw him overboard because he can't swim and would drown! In another strip, Mickey puts on the natural gas in his bedroom while he sleeps, hoping to suffocate to death, but a pesky squirrel breaks in to siphon the gas off to use to fill balloons.

This kept up for a while, until Mickey, while hanging rope on a tree to use as a noose, sees some squirrels laughing at him and realizes how silly all this has been. He decides not to kill himself and instead builds a swing out of the rope. Gottfredson thought it was bizarre when Disney asked him to do the plotline, but apparently Disney had seen it used in a 1920 film starring the comedic actor Harold Lloyd (along with Charlie Chaplin and Buster Keaton, the most popular comedy stars of the silent-film era). Since Lloyd and Mickey shared a lot of the same qualities (both are basic "everyman" characters), Disney felt it would work, and the strips appeared without any complaints from any newspapers.

One can only imagine what Disney thinks of the strips now. They were created by the founder of Disney and published in hundreds of newspapers across the nation almost eighty years ago, but I bet they would be considered far too risqué for Disney today—which is an interesting dichotomy, no?

CARL BARKS, NOTED earlier as the most famous Walt Disney comic artist of all time, very nearly did not become a comic book artist at all.

Barks was raised in Oregon, on a wheat ranch, from which he and his family would move to and from, following his father's attempts at different ventures, all of which would fail. All the time they were traveling, Barks was practicing drawing, and when he was old enough to leave home, he did so, working various odd jobs while submitting cartoons at night. He would even draw cartoons for some of the racier men's magazines before finally traveling to Minnesota in 1931 to take up a steady job drawing cartoons for the *Calgary Eye-Opener*. He ultimately became the editor of the magazine but left in 1935 to go work for Walt Disney's animation studios.

Barks would work for the studios for seven long years, during which time he churned out about thirty-six Donald Duck shorts. In the early 1940s, working on collaborations was slowly driving Barks mad, but he still might not have left the studios if it had not been for something as simple as air-conditioning.

The air-conditioning at the studios caused Barks's sinuses to act up, and he might have stuck out the sinus problems if he loved his job, and he might have stuck out the job if he did not have the sinus problems, but the combination was too great, so Barks quit. He prepared himself to live a life as a chicken farmer (as he and his second wife opened up a chicken farm east of Los Angeles).

When he was settled in, he contacted Western Publishing to see if it was interested in him pitching a new series of comic characters. The company turned him down but did tell him it needed someone to do some Donald Duck comic book stories for *Walt Disney's Comics and Stories*. Barks started working on the series and did not stop for the next twenty-five years—even past his retirement! After his retirement, Barks was so famous around the world (and so respected by Disney) that Disney gave him permission to produce oil-painting versions of famous scenes from his comics. Those paintings would soon each be worth a miniature fortune, with prints of the paintings selling for thousands of dollars. When he died in 2000, at the age of ninety-nine, Barks was mourned throughout the world.

Imagine if Disney Studios had simply fixed the air-conditioning?

KARL KRØYER WAS a prominent Danish inventor who established a firm of inventors and engineers that developed solutions to various problems. His most notable invention occurred during World War II. When food was being rationed, Krøyer developed new methods of food production, specifically sugar. He invented the continuous glucose process, which he patented as Total Sugar.

In 1964 the freighter *Al-Kuwait* sunk off the shores of Kuwait. Within the *Al-Kuwait* were several thousand sheep. Once drowned, the dead sheep would eventually contaminate the water, which was Kuwait's primary source of drinking water. Therefore the ship needed to be raised as quickly as possible, and there was no floating crane available.

The ship was insured by a Dutch company, and it engaged Krøyer's firm to help. One of his young employees came up with the notion that entrapped air could possibly raise the boat. The employee demonstrated by using polystyrol (which is used in heat insulation). An airlift was sent from Berlin to Kuwait with twenty-seven million polystyrol pellets, weighing sixty-five tons. It raised the ship, saving the insurance company over a million dollars in insurance costs.

Krøyer then went on to successfully patent the process in England (GB 1070600) and Germany (DE1247893) but was denied a patent in the Netherlands. The Dutch patent office apparently turned him down because of nothing less than a Carl Barks comic!

When applying for a patent, you must prove that the patent is a "novel" idea—that no one else has come up with the same idea already. When someone has come up with something before you, it is referred to as "prior art." So as long as it has been publicly described in the past, you cannot patent it, even if the prior idea was not patented.

In this incident, the prior art was a Carl Barks story in *Walt Disney's Comics and Stories* #104, in 1949. In the story, Uncle Scrooge's yacht has sunk, and Donald and nephews Huey, Dewey, and Louie raise the boat by filling the yacht with Ping-Pong balls through a tube. Essentially, it is the same process Krøyer used in 1964 (Barks's

© Walt Disney Productions

Ping-Pong-ball process was tested out on a 2004 episode of the television program *MythBusters*—it worked!).

The story is often told that the idea came *from* the comic book, but all the parties involve deny that, and Krøyer was forty-five when the comic was released (although the younger employee may have been the right age to have read it).

The papers for the patent application were destroyed in a fire years ago, so it is difficult to prove that the comic is the specific reason why the patent was denied. However, recently the Netherlands Patent Office issued a statement confirming that it is, in fact, why the patent was denied.

Barks often made a point of trying to make the science in his comics as realistic as possible, so it is not that surprising that something he came up with actually worked.

CARL BARKS'S SCIENTIFIC genius did not only manifest itself in the world of engineering. In 1944, in *Walt Disney's Comics and Stories #44*, Barks made Donald Duck the first duck (or man, see page 204) to discover the chemical compound methylene!

Methylene is a divalent hydrocarbon group that is derived from methane, specifically the carbene CH_2. Carbenes are highly reactive organic molecules with a divalent carbon atom with only six valence electrons. Whether you understand any of the preceding or not, suffice it to say that chemists do understand it, and according to chemistry experts, Barks used methylene in a story in *Walt Disney's Comics and Stories* #44.

In the tale, titled "The Mad Chemist," Donald Duck is hit on the head, and the resulting injury makes him a genius when it comes to chemicals. He mixes together a group of various chemicals in jars to form Duckmite, the most ghastly explosive ever cooked up by man (note that Donald oddly refers to himself as "man"). At one point in the story, Donald references a number of chemicals, and one of the chemicals is CH_2!

A technical article discussing methylene then appeared in a text called *Carbene Chemistry*, and the article cites the appearance of CH_2 in the Barks story as being over a decade ahead of where chemists currently were in the discussion of methylene. The discussion of CH_2 at all in a story in 1944 even predated the discovery of how to prove the *existence* of the chemical intermediate methylene.

Another chemist noted that while, yes, carbenes could not exist in the jars the way that Donald was mixing them in the comic story, they can be made to react with other substances, which real chemical scientists had not thought to try at the time of Barks's strip.

So, without really trying, Barks was a step ahead of the entire field of chemistry! I suppose we are all lucky that Barks never turned his attention to how to make a nuclear reactor in your basement!

THE FACT THAT George Lucas and Steven Spielberg's character Indiana Jones was at least partially inspired by Carl Barks's classic *Uncle Scrooge* comics is fairly evident. Indiana Jones's globe-trotting searches for lost artifacts are extremely similar to Uncle Scrooge's trips (along with his nephew Donald and Donald's nephews, Huey, Dewey, and Louie). This fact was made quite clear when George

© Walt Disney Productions

Lucas wrote the introduction to the collection of Carl Barks's comics published in 1981, *Walt Disney's Uncle Scrooge McDuck: His Life and Times*, and spoke directly about the influence the Barks stories had on both Spielberg and himself.

An oft-repeated but less clear-cut story is that Lucas and Spielberg's famous rolling-boulder scene in *Raiders of the Lost Ark* was an homage to a Carl Barks's comic story. The Barks scene in question appears in "The Seven Cities of Cibola," from *Uncle Scrooge #7*, in which the Beagle Boys, just like Indiana Jones, remove an idol from a pedestal, tripping a lever that sets off a trap that releases a giant boulder down upon them.

That this is an homage is quite often passed off as an undisputed fact, but, really, while the scene certainly bears a resemblance to the famous rolling-boulder scene at the beginning of *Raiders of the Lost Ark*, it is not a straight reproduction by any measure. For instance, the boulders are vastly different sizes and fall in completely different manners. So it is surprising that histories of Barks have always referred to this as though the echo were explicit, but never with a cited source from Lucas or Spielberg.

Luckily, Edward Summer was able to give direct confirmation that the scene was, indeed, influenced by Barks's work. Summer was a friend of Lucas, and it was Summer (along with *Star Wars* producer Gary Kurtz) who put together the aforementioned Barks collection and got Lucas to do the introduction. Each of the stories that appeared in the collection was remastered, including being re-colored. At one point in the production of the collection, Lucas and Summer were talking, and the specific comic that was being prepared for the book was "The Seven Cities of Cibola." Lucas told the editor plainly that the boulder scene in *Raider of the Lost Ark* was a conscious homage to "The Seven Cities of Cibola."

The editor of the collection, who is also a contemporary of Lucas, seems to be a reliable source of information. So yes, the rolling-boulder scene in *Raiders of the Lost Ark* is an homage to a Carl Barks *Uncle Scrooge* comic book. Summer, though, notes that the movie was filled with homages to a number of different sources, so while the boulder scene was a nod to Barks's *Uncle Scrooge*, it could have also been nodding to any number of other works as well, all at the same time.

THE WALT DISNEY corporation has always been very aggressive in the protection of its trademarks, and that was the case when it got involved in the production of the Marvel comic book *Howard the Duck*, which it felt was too close in appearance to its Donald Duck character. Whatever Disney's feelings the level of involvement Marvel allowed Disney is extremely surprising (not to mention disappointing).

Howard the Duck first appeared in a Man-Thing story as a throwaway gag, but creator Steve Gerber liked him enough to bring him back and soon gave him a backup story in *Giant-Size Man-Thing #2* (one of the more sexually suggestive comic book names), and after Marvel saw a decent amount of popular support, Howard gained his own series in 1976 with *Howard the Duck #1.*

The comic is about a talking duck from another world, who is stuck on Earth and gets involved in a series of comical misadventures along with his girlfriend, model-actress Beverly Switzer. The series quickly became a cult hit and even spun off a newspaper strip for a year. Steve Gerber left the series in 1978 over a dispute regarding his rights as the creator of Howard. The series continued without Gerber, but as he was the driving force behind the book, it did not work that well, and after four issues, it relaunched as a black-and-white magazine. This, too, did not last long (only nine issues), and the character disappeared until George Lucas made a box-office flop starring the character.

After Gerber left the book, Disney contacted Marvel about the look of Howard. Disney felt that Howard too closely resembled Donald Duck, and it wanted Marvel to change his appearance.

Amazingly, Marvel agreed to a settlement in which a Disney artist did a redesign of Howard (one of the major points was that

Howard had to wear pants) and Marvel had to agree to stick to that design.

This was an issue when Gerber finally returned to the character in 2002, for a story in Marvel's "mature readers only" MAX line of comics. Gerber disliked the current look of Howard so asked the artist of the new series, Glenn Fabry, to attempt a redesign. It was then that he learned that, according to the deal, Marvel could not even attempt its own redesign. It was Disney's design or nothing! Ger-

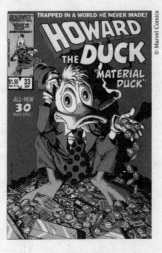

ber was, expectedly, outraged and came up with an idea to get around the rules. Yes, they could not change Howard the Duck's ducklike appearance, but there was nothing saying that they could not make him a different animal! So in each issue of the six-issue series, Gerber had Fabry draw Howard as a different animal. The very first animal was, in "honor" of Disney, a mouse.

Marvel must have managed to rework the agreement (or else decided to risk it), because in 2007 it released a new *Howard the Duck* miniseries with a brand-new design of Howard by the book's artist, Juan Bobillo.

WITH THE AMOUNT of litigation Disney is routinely involved in over its trademark protection, it is remarkable to note that it has allowed the University of Oregon to use Donald Duck as its mascot for over sixty years!

The Oregon Ducks' first school nickname was the Webfoots, a term referring to fishermen from the area during the nineteenth century. Eventually, Webfoots was shortened to, and then kept as, Ducks.

This was especially prominent during the 1920s and '30s, when the school began bringing a live duck named Puddles to its games as the school mascot. This practice was objected to by the Humane Society and was finally canceled in the early 1940s. By that time, depictions of the duck had already begun to proliferate in school newspapers when discussing the football team, and the duck began to be drawn looking like Donald Duck. Eventually, the team logo was, essentially, Donald Duck. In the late 1940s, the Walt Disney Company began to notice—and disapproved.

Luckily, Oregon athletic director Leo Harris was close friends with an employee at Disney and managed to set up a meeting with Walt Disney himself. Harris flew to Los Angeles to ask Disney to allow the school to continue using Donald as its mascot. Disney agreed, and the two shook on the deal (without, though, formalizing the agreement through a written contract). At the time, Harris, Disney, and two other men posed for a photograph together, squatting behind Puddles.

Oregon continued to use Donald for the next couple of decades, until Disney passed away in 1966. At this point, Oregon was quite mindful of the fact that it did not actually have a written contract with Disney. When the company asked about the deal, all it had to prove it was, well, the photograph!

Ultimately, Disney decided that the photo was fairly good evidence of Walt's intent regarding the school's mascot, so it eventually signed a written contract allowing Oregon to maintain Donald as its mascot, with the caveat that it was only for school functions, and any merchandise bearing Donald could only be sold in Oregon, with the profits split between the university and Disney.

While such a deal made sense to Oregon at the time, by the turn of the twenty-first century, such an agreement was pretty limiting, as sales of college football merchandise was now a national enterprise. Around this same time, Oregon coincidentally introduced a new, additional duck mascot (designed by Nike, which has a very close relationship with the University of Oregon, as Nike cofounder and president Phil Knight is an alumnus, and the other cofounder was a track-and-field coach for Oregon), which it said was just an attempt to have a separate, more agile mascot to accompany Donald. That might be the case, or perhaps it was a hint to Disney that it would be prepared to replace Donald if the contract was not renegotiated.

In any case, a new agreement was eventually signed, but the terms were sealed, and since no new merchandise with Donald has popped up, it appears as though the terms did not change that much.

11

VARIOUS COMIC BOOK COMPANIES

During the 1940s, postal-service laws required that whenever a publication began a new volume it must reapply for a new permit allowing its subscriptions to be sent by second-class mail (since 1996 publications sent via second-class mail are called periodicals). Naturally, every time you apply for a new permit, you have to pay the fee. Magazines generally could afford such a fee, so they were fine with starting a new volume each year. Comic companies, however, did not like to pay this fee, and that is why numbering on comic books stays the same from the beginning. And it is why *Action Comics* hit #861 in June 2008 instead of being Vol. 80, No. 6. This avoidance of renumbering has led to some interesting scenarios when it comes to naming comic books.

Companies would often simply change the name of the comic when they changed the lead feature, since any benefit from starting over with a new volume number was outweighed by the detriment of having to pay the new fee (in addition, first issues did not have the same appeal back then). For instance, Quality Comics' *Kid Eternity* was about a young man who accidentally died seventy-five years too early, so Heaven sent him back to Earth to live out the remaining seventy-five years as a superhero with the ability to call upon any historical figure he wanted by saying, "Eternity!" *Kid Eternity* lasted eighteen issues, at which point it was retitled *Buccaneers*, and became a comic book about pirates, the first issue of which was #19.

However, while comic book companies could try to change the name of the comic to avoid paying the fee, they had to be discreet, because the U.S. Postal Service certainly did not want to be played for suckers. Quality Comics also had a comic called *Ken Shannon*, about a private eye (who had a tough-as-nails secretary furnished with great dialogue like, "Oooh, lovely, Ken! Hit him again!"). That, somehow, did not sell too well, so after ten issues, Quality retitled the book *Gabby*, making the comic a teen comedy à la Archie. The U.S. Postal Service was hip to Quality's tricks, though, and after one issue, it was both forced to pay the fee and to number the book correctly (so *Gabby* went from #11 to #2). EC Comics had this in mind, undoubtedly, when it was involved in one of the strangest series of retitlings imaginable!

In 1947 EC Comics debuted a rare superhero comic book (it almost entirely eschewed the superhero genre) called *Moon Girl* (the first issue was titled *Moon Girl and the Prince*, but it became *Moon Girl* from #2 on). Moon Girl was essentially the same as Wonder Woman: she was from another land and won a contest to leave her kingdom to go fight crime in America. The title was not a huge success, and with issue #7, EC decided to change the book to reflect the hot trend in comics at the time—crime comics! So with #7 the book became *Moon Girl Fights Crime*. Two issues later, EC changed its mind again, and this time it decided to make the comic a romance book. The title was now stretched well beyond credulity to become *A Moon, a Girl . . . Romance*. Even this last change did not do much for the title, and it was canceled after #12.

Retitling kept up well into the 1960s, though, as Marvel retitled all its anthologies rather than starting all over, so *Thor* took over the numbering of *Journey into Mystery*, *The Incredible Hulk* took over the numbering of *Tales to Astonish*, *Doctor Strange* assumed the numbering of *Strange Tales*, and *Captain America* inherited the numbering of *Tales of Suspense*.

The bias against low numbers also continued in the 1960s, as the #1 was intentionally left off of the cover of the first issue of *Justice League of America*, because DC did not want readers to know it was a first issue. This first issue of *Justice League* sold significantly fewer copies than the issues after it, because old, at the time, meant proven goodness, while new comics begged the question, "Will this be good?"

EC COMICS' DESIRE to save money was also the basis for a memorable encounter between its publisher Bill Gaines and legendary science fiction author Ray Bradbury.

EC Comics was the brainchild of Gaines, who allowed Harry Donenfeld to buy him out of All-American Publications (in the merger that created the DC Comics we know today). Gaines started Educational Comics with one title that he retained from the deal, *Picture Stories from the Bible*. Gaines's plan was to market a line of comics about science, history, and the Bible to schools and churches. At the time he died, in a boating accident in 1947, Gaines's company was floundering. Upon his father's death, his son, Bill, was forced to take over the family business. Relying heavily on the existing editors, Al Feldstein and Harvey Kurtzman, Gaines set out to remake the company. Now calling itself Entertaining Comics (that change might have started right before the elder Gaines's death), the company dedicated itself to high-quality stories in the horror, suspense, science fiction, military fiction, and crime fiction genres.

Noted titles from this time include *Tales from the Crypt*, *The Vault of Horror*, *The Haunt of Fear*, *Two-Fisted Tales*, *Crime SuspenStories*, *Weird Science*, and *Weird Fantasy*.

Putting out so many books often called for shortcuts, and one was taken when Gaines and Feldstein swiped a bit from a Ray Bradbury story for a 1951 comic. The story, "A Strange Undertaking . . . ," mirroring Bradbury's "The Handler," appeared in *Haunt of Fear* #6. Feldstein made a few more borrowings after that, but it was one year later in *Weird Fantasy* #13 that caught Ray Bradbury's eye (and, presumably, a bit of his ire).

The story, titled "Home to Stay!" was cobbled together from two Bradbury stories, "Kaleidoscope" and "The Rocket Man." Now, some writers would react to their work being swiped by getting angry. Bradbury, however, decided to play it a different way and sent the following brilliant letter to Gaines in 1952: "Just a note to remind you of an oversight. You have not as yet sent on the check for $50.00 to cover the use of secondary rights on my two stories THE ROCKET MAN and KALEIDOSCOPE. . . . I feel this was probably overlooked in the general confusion of office work, and look forward to your payment in the near future."

Gaines was no fool—he quickly sent the money, along with a cordial response, and pretty soon Bradbury was authorizing EC Comics to do official adaptations of his stories. The covers of *Weird Science* and *Weird Fantasy* posted in bold letters that they featured official Ray Bradbury stories. These became quite a draw for EC's science fiction titles.

Sadly, due to the theories of Dr. Wertham (described on page 67) and the ensuing congressional hearings (at which EC Comics' horror comics were specifically highlighted), the Comics Code Authority was formed. The Comics Code was devastating to EC Comics, and ultimately led to the dissolution of the company. Luckily, Gaines had begun producing a satirical comic book called *Mad*, mostly as a pet project for Kurtzman. In 1955, in an effort to keep Kurtzman, who had gotten an offer to take over the magazine *PARADE*, Gaines turned

Every issue of *Weird Science* after EC began doing official Bradbury adaptations included these banners, as seen here on the cover to *Weird Science* #18.

Mad into a magazine. In that form, it became a cultural institution and, because it was a magazine, fell outside the purview of the Comics Code—though that was not the impetus of the format change; Kurtzman's departure was).

QUALITY COMICS WAS the brainchild of Everett M. "Busy" Arnold, a printer who saw firsthand the demand for comic books in the 1940s and so set out to form his own comic book company. The name of the company matched its product—Arnold had a great many of the most notable artists of the period working for him, including Jack Cole, who created *Plastic Man* for Quality; Will Eisner, who created a number of superheroes for Quality and also had a deal with Arnold to publish his popular *Spirit* newspaper strip; and Reed Crandall, most noted for the work about to be discussed.

During the 1940s, books would be assembled in a rather ramshackle manner, especially when dealing with comic packagers (groups that would create ready-to-print comic book stories to sell to comic book companies looking to quickly put out content). The birth of *Blackhawk* was a result of that disorderly creative process.

The stars of *Blackhawk* were the Blackhawk Squadron, a small team of ace pilots during World War II. They came from various countries but fought together in matching planes. Each character was known by a one-word name, like Andre or Chuck or Chop-Chop (who went from being a fairly offensive Chinese parody to being a more realistic character by the end of the series). The series was created by Will Eisner, Chuck Cuidera, and Bob Powell, but writer-artist Reed Crandall was the name most associated with the series. It was a big hit, especially overseas (as each country had a hero to root for), and it soon spun off a radio show, a novelization, and a film serial. It had its own title, *Blackhawk*, but got its start in 1941 as the lead feature in *Military Comics* #1. However, amusingly enough, *Blackhawk* was actually based on another comic—a comic that made its debut as a backup story to Blackhawk!

As noted above, Jack Cole was the creator of Plastic Man, who is a wonderfully hilarious comedic character. So in 1941, he came up with a comedic war comic, called "Death Patrol." The story involved a disparate group of criminals who escaped from prison and snuck aboard a plane owned by millionaire Del van Dyne. They were going to hijack the plane, but change their mind when they learn he was headed to England, where they would be free from U.S. law. Once there, though, van Dyne convinces them to help in the war effort, and they ultimately agree, under the theory that being killed fighting the Germans is better than life in prison, hence their colorful name. So they each steal a German plane and fight together as the Death Patrol (their prison uniforms are their team uniform). Well, after handing in the story, the other creators at Quality liked the idea and thought that a more serious version of the story would work well—thus the Blackhawk Squadron was born! After the Blackhawk story was finished, it was determined that it deserved the lead feature and cover spot over "Death Patrol," which is how it was released.

In 1956 Arnold sold Quality to DC, and *Blackhawk* was one of the titles DC continued to publish. "Death Patrol" was not (to date at least), but it can feel some comfort in being the influence for such a long-running series!

As mentioned a few times before, in the early days of comics a popular method for making comic books would be to hire a studio of artists who would "package" (produce) any type of comic for anyone who paid their fee. One of the most notable of these studios was the Eisner-Iger studio, formed by Will Eisner and Robert Iger in 1935.

The pair would deliver a number of series over the next few years, from secret agents to jungle girls to pirates, but in 1939 they received a bizarre job offer. For one of their first (if not the very first) superhero characters, they were asked to rip off Superman!

Many a story has been told about Victor Fox, most of them not very flattering, but in a way Fox's lack of scruples was what made him successful (except when he was indicted in 1929 for mail fraud). When he saw the success of Superman, he hired Eisner to flat out rip off Superman. The resulting character, Wonder Man, debuted in *Wonder Comics* #1, a mere year after Superman's debut (a remarkable turnaround, really).

The issue was notable for being the first copyright lawsuit in comic book history, as National Comics quickly sued Fox and gained an injunction over the use of Wonder Man until the suit was resolved.

Fox had prepared Eisner's testimony for him, but when it came time for him to testify, Eisner told the truth and Fox was sunk. Wonder Man's comic book career ended up being one issue. However, Fox was undaunted, and his company went on to create a number of heroes (most of them unmemorable), with the lone bright spot being Blue Beetle, which he sold to Charlton Comics when Fox went under in the mid-1950s. (Like Quality, when Charlton went under its comics went to DC, which now owns Blue Beetle.)

As MENTIONED (on pages 56–9), Captain Marvel and his related titles were hugely popular during the 1940s, and one of the most notable influences it had apparently was on none other than the King of Rock 'n' Roll himself, Elvis Presley!

Mac Raboy was an intriguing artist. He was a master at portraying lighting, and as a result his panels were dynamic and had a polish that other artists could only dream of achieving. However, such work takes time, so Raboy would often resort to various time-saving techniques to get his books out on time, including using the same panels over and over again.

Still, despite his panel recycling, Raboy's *Captain Marvel Jr.* was a huge success, and is an acclaimed series to this day. The comic was about a younger version of Captain Marvel. Freddy Freeman was a crippled teenager who could transform into a junior version of Captain Marvel, and back, by saying, "Captain Marvel!" becoming, as a result, the only hero who couldn't say his own name without reverting back to his secret identity! Captain Marvel Jr. had a distinctive hairstyle, and apparently Elvis Presley used it as the guide for his famous hairstyle.

In her biography *Elvis and Gladys*, Elaine Dundy wrote that Elvis Presley grew up as a big fan of Captain Marvel Jr. and took the character's hairstyle as his own when he became older. According to Dundy, "Behind Elvis there was another great legend: the metaphysical world of double-identity comic book heroes. Elvis's favorite was Captain Marvel Jr., who looks, in fact, exactly like Elvis will make himself look for the rest of his life." It sounds bizarre, but Elvis was definitely a huge fan of Captain Marvel Jr., and his collection of *Captain Marvel Jr.* comics still sits in Graceland. His hairstyle really does look like Captain Marvel Jr.'s.

© Metro-Goldwyn-Mayer Inc.

Later on, during the Vegas years, Elvis incorporated more Captain Marvel regalia into his look, including the distinctive cape he wore.

IN THE EARLY days of comic books, pretty much any idea could turn out to be the "next big thing." Lev Gleason was one of the few publishers out there who would actually share with his artists the profits of coming up with the next big thing. He told them, "If you come up with something that is a hit, you will make a lot of money." Perhaps inspired by this, two of his editors, Charlie Biro and Bob Wood, came up with an idea that ruled the comics world of the late 1940s and early '50s—crime comics.

When Biro and Wood pitched the idea to Gleason in 1942 (supposedly inspired by an incident where Biro and Wood saw a man with a woman one night at a bar and then saw the next day that the woman was a kidnap victim), he thought it was a great idea and allowed them to turn *Silver Streak Comics* (a standard superhero title) into *Crime Does Not Pay* with issue #22.

The comic was a massive hit, and led to spools of imitators. Years later, though, sales in the crime genre were slowing, and due to the strict new Comics Code installed by the comic publishers the gore of the standard crime comics was toned down and, in fact, even the word *crime* could not be set bigger than the other words in the title! So in 1955, with *Crime Does Not Pay* #147, the series limped into oblivion. It is a real shame, too, that the comic folded at the time, because only a few years later, in 1958, one of the creators of the comic was himself involved in a true crime story!

Comic writer-artist Bob Wood was always involved in the somewhat seedier side of life in New York City, with gambling debts constantly piling up. However, in the summer of 1958 (years after the successful *Crime* franchise he helped create was over), Wood was arrested for killing a woman in a drunken argument.

A cab driver picked Wood up near Gramercy Park in New York, and Wood told the driver that he needed to sleep for a few hours and then he'd throw himself into the river. The cab driver asked if he had killed somebody, and Wood replied that yes, he killed a woman that was giving him a hard time. He told him the room number and told the cabbie to call the story in and earn a few dollars for his troubles.

When the police came to arrest Wood at the Residence Hotel the cabbie drove him to, his suit was so blood soaked that the cops had to lend him a pair of pants to take him to jail. When they went to the room that Wood noted, they found a collection of empty whiskey bottles and a woman in a negligee who had been beaten to death.

Wood pleaded guilty to first-degree manslaughter and served three years in prison. A year after he was released, he ran afoul of the wrong crowd over some unpaid loans and died under suspicious circumstances, likely murder. It was a tragic end to a real tale of crime truly not paying.

OFTEN COMIC BOOK history seems to focus on the atypical, the rare breed of artists who become lasting successes, when really the majority of comic creators during the golden age of comics in the 1940s and '50s have been lost to obscurity. They typically spent their time cobbling together whatever assignments they could get before ultimately being forced to give up on comics entirely. Dick Briefer was such a creator, who stands out now because his work has gained critical appreciation in the decades since he left the comic book field, but at the time Briefer was taking any assignment he could find, including a superhero for Communists!

Briefer broke into the industry working for Eisner-Iger, doing fairly nondescript work. It was not until 1940 that he gained some measure of acclaim (and much more since) for his adaptation of Mary Shelley's *Frankenstein*, which he set in America in the twentieth century, as the story of a horrific rampaging monster (much like the Hulk) actually named Frankenstein. Eventually—like every other character—Frankenstein began fighting the Nazis, and then, in 1945, Briefer did a complete about-face and turned *Frankenstein* into a hilarious humor magazine, with Frankenstein and his fellow monsters having jolly adventures, even calling himself Frank N. Stein! This ended in the late 1940s, and, in an even odder turn of events, the series had a brief revival in the 1950s when horror comics became popular, once again as the horror comic of its beginnings.

Frankenstein was not a big enough hit for Briefer to work on it alone, so Briefer had to look for other work, and at one point in the 1940s he created a hero for the *Daily Worker*, the popular newspaper of the American Communist Party!

Writing as Dick Floyd, Briefer created *Pinky Rankin*, a fairly good-humored character who fought Nazis while also teaching lessons of socialism through repeatedly stressing the power of standing together as one solid social front.

After the *Frankenstein* revival of the 1950s fell flat, Briefer retired from comics and worked in advertising until his death in 1982. Briefer's *Frankenstein* has been reprinted in deluxe formats in recent years, but *Pinky Rankin* has yet to be given the same treatment.

As NOTED ABOVE, the majority of comic book creators during the golden age of the 1940s and '50s ended up spending only a small amount of time in the industry, but because of that, a great many of these creators had popular success in some other form. For instance, Mickey Spillane (author of the popular Mike Hammer series of crime novels) and Patricia Highsmith (author of *The Talented Mr. Ripley* and the ensuing series of Ripley novels) both worked writing comics during the 1940s. One could think of a number of people who might be believable comic book creators, but one person who has recently been reported, in a number of places, as having done comic book work did not, in fact, work in comic books, although he did work in comics period. That person is Academy Award–winning actor Martin Landau!

When he was still a teenager in the late 1940s, Landau, who is from Brooklyn, began working as a cartoonist at the *New York Daily News*, drawing various small illustrations. He then went on to work as an assistant for Gus Edson on the popular comic strip *The Gumps*

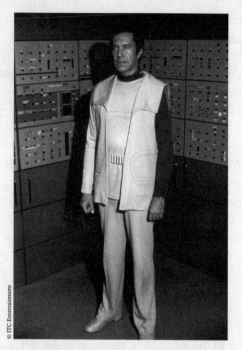

Landau from the 1970s science fiction
series *Space 1999.*

(which was one of the very first continuity strips, telling the story of
an ordinary family from 1917 until the series ended in 1959). However, by the 1950s he was fully pursuing a career as an actor, doing a
number of roles on various television programs (and small film
roles) before finding success on two notable series, *Mission: Impossible* and *Space: 1999.* He soon became a popular film actor, ultimately
winning the Academy Award for Best Supporting Actor in 1994 for
his role in *Ed Wood.*

Most likely, Landau missed out on drawing comic books just by
bad timing. He was born in 1930, so during the big boom of the
1940s he was only an adolescent, and by the time he was of age to

work in comics the industry was in a post–World War II slowdown, eliminating the surplus of jobs of the war era.

It is probably for the best, because if comic books gained Landau, the world of acting would have lost him, and he is far too good of an actor to lose.

EVEN IF MARTIN Landau had worked as a comic book artist, he would not have been nearly as strange of a comic book artist as another actor who did work at Harvey Comics in the 1960s.

Harvey Comics was founded by Alfred Harvey in 1941 and became one of the biggest sellers of comic books for children, popularizing such notable characters as Casper the Friendly Ghost, Baby Huey, and Little Audrey and creating characters like Richie Rich, Little Dot, and Hot Stuff. They were massively popular throughout the 1960s, but while the Harvey characters continue to be popular in other media, the company ceased publishing comics in 1986 (with a brief comeback in the late 1990s).

At one point in the 1960s, Ruth Leon, an artist for Harvey, brought in a young artist from France, and editor Sid Jacobson gave him a few pages to ink, which he did before leaving New York to try his luck as an actor. The young artist's name? Hervé Villechaize.

Hervé Villechaize had proportionate dwarfism from birth, and took solace from the taunts of schoolmates by losing himself in painting. After graduating from art college in France, he traveled to New York, where he lived the life of an artist, learning English from television and working as an artist and photographer. It was then that he worked for Harvey Comics. He also began to act in plays and soon moved to Hollywood to pursue a film career, which was highlighted by his turn as Nick Nack in the James Bond film *The Man with the Golden Gun*. Soon he costarred in the hit television series *Fantasy Island* as Tattoo, the assistant of the island's owner, Mr. Roarke.

© Viacom, Inc.

After leaving the show over a salary dispute, Villechaize's life was difficult.

In 1993 he committed suicide, just as he was about to gain a regular role as the sidekick on the upcoming Cartoon Network series *Space Ghost Coast to Coast*, based on the work of comic book artist Alex Toth.

IT WOULD NOT be much of an exaggeration, if one at all, to call Héctor Germán Oesterheld the greatest comic book writer Argentina ever saw. In fact, it might not be a stretch to say that he was the greatest comic book writer South America ever saw.

After becoming a popular comic book writer during the 1940s and '50s, Oesterheld was able to launch his own comic book company with his brother Jorge in 1957. The company was called Ediciones Frontera. The company launched two hugely successful comic books, which Oesterheld wrote many stories for, and they were *Hora Cero* (Zero Hour) and *Frontera* (Frontier).

For *Hora Cero*, Oesterheld worked with legendary comic artist Hugo Pratt on the popular "Ernie Pike." Ernie Pike was a war journalist, likely modeled after Ernie Pyle, and Oesterheld used the comic to express his disgust with war.

It was also in *Hora Cero* that Oesterheld developed perhaps his most popular work, the time-travel science fiction epic, "El Eternauta," with artist Francisco Solano López. The series dealt with an alien invasion of Earth, during which a deadly snow falls over Argentina, wiping out most of the population. Equipped with protective gear, small groups of resistance fighters try to regain their world from the invaders. In an attempt to escape, the main character, Juan Salvo, and his wife and daughter are instead hurtled through time, each to a different time continuum. Salvo then has to search through various alternate realities to find his wife and daughter.

An economic depression in the 1960s caused Oesterheld's company to close down, but Oesterheld continued to write for other comic companies. Eventually, his work took on more and more of a political bent, culminating in perhaps his greatest political work, a biography of Che Guevara titled *Vida del Che*, which came out in 1968, with artwork by Alberto and Enrique Breccia.

In 1976 there was a military coup in Argentina. In protest, Oesterheld began work on a continuation of "El Eternauta," this time showing a future Argentina ruled by a dictatorship. In addition, Oesterheld (and his family) joined the antigovernment group the Montoneros, whose existence was outlawed by the government. Oesterheld mailed in his "El Eternauta" scripts from secret locations.

Late in 1976, after already seeing all his daughters arrested, Oesterheld too was arrested by the government, and no one ever saw him after Christmas of that year.

There is a famous quote (perhaps apocryphal) concerning Oesterheld, which was supposedly told to an Italian journalist, Alberto Ongaro, in 1979 when he was inquiring about Oesterheld's disappearance: "We did away with him because he wrote the most beautiful story of Che Guevara ever done."

In the late 1990s, a wonderful documentary called *H.G.O.* was made about Oesterheld's life and tragic death.

AFTER BEING OUSTED as the editor in chief of Marvel Comics, Jim Shooter decided to start his own comic book company, Valiant. He got the company started off by first doing a number of tie-in books with the World Wrestling Federation and Nintendo. Then, as a basis for the new universe of characters he was creating, he licensed a number of characters from Western Publishing's defunct Gold Key line of comics: Magnus, Robot Fighter (a man in the future who, well, fights robots); Dr. Solar, Man of the Atom (a hero who wields energy powers); and Turok, Son of Stone (a Native American who hunts dinosaurs).

After establishing the universe, Shooter began introducing new characters. One, who received his own book, was X-O Manowar, a barbarian from the fifth century who is given a futuristic and powerful suit of alien armor then brought to the twentieth century and forced to make his way in the world. Marvel took issue with the title of the book, apparently feeling (perhaps not too unreasonably) that any comic with an *X* so prominently displayed would be confused with its *X-Men* comics.

Shooter obviously disagreed with his former employers, but to hedge his bets he played an interesting trick, along with fellow former Marvel writer Steve Englehart, who he had hired to write some of the early Valiant titles. In his creator-owned title in the 1980s, Englehart had created and trademarked a character named X-Caliber. Marvel attempted to purchase the character from Englehart in the late 1980s, but he turned down the offer, so Marvel instead launched a book called *Excalibur* instead of *X-Calibur*, which was the original hope. So when Shooter was approached by Marvel over *X-O Manowar*, he licensed the name X-Caliber from Englehart and had him guest star in *X-O Manowar*. Marvel backed down, and eventually Shooter agreed to stop using the name X-Caliber and changed the name when Valiant did a trade collection of *X-O Manowar*.

MARVEL WAS BLAMED for the loss of another prominent independent comic of the 1990s, but the actual reason was much more typical (if disappointing).

John Byrne was one of the most popular comic book artists of the 1980s, doing a number of popular series for Marvel. In 1991, after a deal failed to materialize with DC Comics, Byrne debuted his series *John Byrne's Next Men* for Mike Richardson's Dark Horse Comics.

The series starred a group of genetically engineered young men and women with various superpowers who escape from custody and go on the run sometime in the near future (at least it was the near future when the comic debuted in the early 1990s). The book was typical for its time period in the way that it took a more mature look at superheroes and how they would affect a fairly realistic world. Also, being at Dark Horse,

Byrne had more freedom to use language and content that would be considered too adult for DC or Marvel.

© Marvel Comics

The series was acclaimed and sold well at first, but in 1995 it ended with #30 and a cliff-hanger. There were rumors going around at the time that Marvel was complaining about the book, feeling that *Next Men* was too similar of a title to its *X-Men* series, especially with the at-first-glance similarities between the characters.

However, that was not the case (and Byrne using his own name as part of the title was likely a purposeful move to ensure that the title was clearly different). The title folded because Byrne decided to take a break to do some mainstream work since sales of the book had dropped. Byrne's intent was to leave, do some higher-paying mainstream work, and then return to the series. Little did he know that the bottom proceeded to fall out of the comic book industry during the late 1990s, and by the end of the decade a series like *Next Men* would not be financially possible.

Byrne has not returned to the characters since then, but it was recently announced that IDW Publishing, a company Byrne is doing some work for at the moment, will be releasing trade collections of the series.

WHEN IMAGE COMICS began, Todd McFarlane might have been the most popular of all the original Image artists. His debut title for Image, *Spawn*, about a government assassin who dies but returns as a demon from hell determined to use his evil powers for good, was a monster hit, with the first issue selling over a million copies.

Over the years, McFarlane has drawn more attention for his actions outside his comic (which he stopped drawing himself after a few years). These include his popular toy company (McFarlane Toys is noted for the extremely high quality of its sculpting and is used by many companies to create licensed toys, including most popular American sports) and his obsession with sports (highlighted by his purchase of the baseball Mark McGwire hit for his seventieth home run in 1998 and the ball Barry Bonds hit for his seventy-third home run in 2001: three million dollars for McGwire's ball, considerably less for Bonds's).

One thing McFarlane probably does not want to be reminded of is his legal battles. The most notable occurred because of something that happened in his comic (and came about due to his love of sports).

McFarlane is Canadian and a major fan of the National Hockey League (NHL), and once even part owner of the Edmonton Oilers, so in the pages of *Spawn*, he introduced a mob enforcer named Antonio "Tony Twist" Twistelli. Anthony "Tony" Twist was an NHL player known for being a fierce "enforcer"; that is, a player who makes sure that the star players on his team are protected from being roughed up by opposing teams' players. Twist sued McFarlane over the character, claiming McFarlane was attempting to profit off Twist's likeness. In 2004 a jury awarded Twist fifty million dollars in damages. McFarlane appealed, but after two appeals, the judgment was upheld in 2006. McFarlane declared bankruptcy to deal with the settlement, but as of today his company is still around, making toys and hoping to produce a second film based on the Spawn character.

ANOTHER COMPANY THAT was involved in a legal matter involving names was Archie Comics, which drew quite a bit of attention (and more than a bit of derision) for a cease and desist letter it sent in 1998—telling a family to pull down a Web site called veronica.org.

The Internet has been a difficult area in which to establish hard-and-fast rules for the protection of intellectual property, such as trademarks. So-called cybersquatting has become a major issue online, with people registering domain names that they feel companies will later want to use and then attempting to sell the companies the rights to the domain name for exorbitant fees, or using a domain name that would likely bring in people interested in a particular company or organization and then using the Web site to insult that company or organization. A notable case of the latter would be when People for the Ethical Treatment of Animals (PETA) won a lawsuit against a man who registered peta.org for a site called People Eating Tasty Animals.

However, that was not the case when David Sams registered the domain name veronica.org in honor of his infant daughter named Veronica. In 1998 he received a cease and desist letter from Archie Comics, telling him to give up the Web site, because it was a trademark of Archie Comics (which already owned the domain name veronica.com).

Rather than give in, Sams responded with a letter to Archie Comics explaining his dissatisfaction with its behavior. He made it public, and it soon became an embarrassing news story for Archie. It is similar to an incident in 1998 where the Prema Toy Company sent a cease and desist letter to what turned out to be a twelve-year-old boy who registered pokey.org for his personal Web site because that was his nickname. Prema wanted it because of its character Pokey from the Gumby toy line. In both cases, the public outcry led to a quick withdrawal of the letters (in the case of pokey.org, the creator of Pokey even wrote to complain).

Amusingly, veronica.org is, as of March 2008, not currently registered by anyone.

* * *

STRANGELY ENOUGH, THIS was not the only instance when Archie pursued legal action over the use of a character's name. Even stranger is that the second instance also involved Veronica! Luckily, this case had a happy ending for both parties.

Lisa Marie Origliasso and Jessica Louise Origliasso were born in Australia, to Italian parents, on Christmas Day 1984. The twins grew up interested in show business and appeared on television in the 2001 Australian children's series, *Cybergirl.* When they turned eighteen years old, Jessica received a guitar, and the two began writing and performing songs together, eventually forming a band called Teal. The Bell Hughes Music Group (BHMG) took an interest in the girls, and it was around this time that they changed the group's name. Since both girls were attractive, black-haired teens, people used to call them the Veronicas, after Archie's girlfriend in the *Archie* comic book series. That is the name they began to perform under (although the girls were ambivalent about the name because it gives the impression that they are a pop duo, while they maintain they are a full rock band).

Archie took issue with the use of the name and filed a suit against the band for trademark infringement. Luckily, this time, the two reached an agreement. Rather than fight, they signed a deal to cross-promote each other. The girls appeared in *Veronica* #167, along with a card that featured a code for a download of a Veronicas music single.

© Archie Comics, image courtesy of Rik Offenberger

Since their first appearance, the Veronicas have become popular guest stars in the comics, appearing numerous times, even in *Archie's 65th Anniversary Bash* (which was given out on Free Comic Book Day 2007). Meanwhile, the Veronicas have released two well-received albums, *The Secret Life of . . .* (2005) and *Hook Me Up* (2007).

It's always nice to hear of an intellectual property case having such a happy ending.

IN 2001, WHEN Ben and Ray Lai created their *Radix* series about a group of armored operatives, for Image Comics, they could foresee a number of options for their book: It could be a surprise hit, or it could come and go without much fanfare. It could serve as a gateway to future work at Marvel or DC (it did, in fact, get them work at Marvel on the *Thor* comic book series). What they could not have foreseen was their work being used by the Massachusetts Institute of Technology (MIT) to receive a fifty-million-dollar grant from the United States Army, and yet that is exactly what happened!

© Ben and Ray Lai

Edwin L. Thomas, director of MIT's Institute for Soldier Nanotechnologies, headed up the grant proposal, which was to develop a supersoldier armor that would enhance strength and allow for some form of invisibility as well as many other fantastic features. Thomas featured on the cover of the proposal a drawing from the Lais' comic series *Radix*, as an example of what the armor would look like.

Thomas claims that his daughter told him that she drew the image, and in fact the image is credited to H. Thomas. However, even after being challenged by the Lais, at first MIT would not apologize, claiming it was "innocent use." The Lai brothers felt that it damaged their reputation, as it appeared as though they copied MIT, while it was the other way around, and that it could damage their attempts at perhaps having *Radix* optioned for film or television.

Ultimately, MIT issued an apology, and that essentially finished matters (although the Lais kept holding out for more), but in a way it is almost a compliment (while still being quite wrong on MIT's part) to know that one's artwork was a part of a grant proposal for over fifty million dollars!

Recommended Reading

Here is a list of sources for, and interesting further reading related to, each chapter of this book.

First off, though, here are five good general resources:

News from Me (http://www.newsfromme.com/): Mark Evanier's Web site, packed to the brim with helpful information.

Alter Ego: Roy Thomas's monthly magazine about comic book history from Two-Morrows Publishing.

Back Issue: Michael Eury's bimonthly magazine about more recent comic book history, also from TwoMorrows Publishing.

The Comic Book Makers: Joe Simon's book about comic book history—partially his own memories of the business and partially objective history.

Men of Tomorrow: Geeks, Gangsters, and the Birth of the Comic Book: Gerard Jones's thrilling work investigating the early history of comic books.

CHAPTER ONE: SUPERMAN

The Superman Homepage (http://www.supermanhomepage.com): An amazing resource, it provided most of the information for the Superman as a spy story.

The Speeding Bullet (http://www.thespeedingbullet.com): An archive of Superman comic strips.

Who's Whose (http://www.supermanartists.comic.org): Bob Hughes's amazing resource of which comic book artist drew which comic.

Superman Radio Show (http://www.redboots.net/sradio/radio_show.htm): A resource about the Superman radio program.

CHAPTER TWO: BATMAN

Dial B for Blog (http://dialbforblog.com): A great comic book Web site that is fun and informative and has some good information about the early history of Batman and Bob Kane.

Silver Age Comics (http://sacomics.blogspot.com): A site about comics from the silver age, including an excellent section on Batman's early violent history.

CHAPTER THREE: DC COMICS MISCELLANEA

On *National v. Fawcett* (http://www.worldfamouscomics.com/law/back20001024 .shtml): Here comic legal expert Bob Ingersoll takes an in-depth look at the case between National/DC Comics and Fawcett Comics over whether Captain Marvel infringed on Superman.

"The Transmigration of Flex Mentallo" (http://www.highway-62.com/blog/ archives/2003/07/the_transmigration_of_flex_men.htm): A good look at the Flex Mentallo case on Matt Maxwell's Highway 62 blog.

The Unofficial Guide to the DC Universe (http://www.dcuguide.com/): Just what the title of the site says it is.

CHAPTER FOUR: THE FANTASTIC FOUR

"The Religion of the Thing" (http://www.adherents.com/lit/comics/Thing.html): An in-depth examination of the Thing's Judaism and its revelation.

Kirby: King of Comics: Mark Evanier's recent Jack Kirby biography, featuring a lot of excellent information about his work on *The Fantastic Four*.

CHAPTER FIVE: SPIDER-MAN

Ditko Looked Up (http://www.ditko.comics.org/): Blake Bell's impressive Web site devoted to Steve Ditko.

"Randy Schueller's Brush with Comic History" (http://goodcomics.comicbook resources.com/2007/05/16/randy-schuellers-brush-with-comic-history): Schueller tells the story about how Marvel bought his idea for Spider-Man getting a black costume.

Spiderfan.org (http://www.spiderfan.org/): Amazing Web reference page for Spider-Man fans.

CHAPTER SIX: THE INCREDIBLE HULK

Doug's Incredible Hulk Comic Page (http://www.hulkcomicpage.com/): Good Web resource for information about the Hulk.

CHAPTER SEVEN: CAPTAIN AMERICA

Simon and Kirby (http://kirbymuseum.org/blogs/simonandkirby/): Harry Mendryk's blog dedicated to the works of the duo of Joe Simon and Jack Kirby, including Captain America.

Steve Englehart's Web site (http://www.steveenglehart.com/): The writer talks about his past projects, including his Captain America run.

CHAPTER EIGHT: THE X-MEN

UncannyXMen.net (http://www.uncannyxmen.net/): The premier Web resource for X-Men information.

CHAPTER NINE: MARVEL COMICS MISCELLANEA

It's BobRo the Answer Man! (http://www.comicsbulletin.com/bobro/archive.htm): Now defunct, but still a useful comic book resource featuring longtime comic book professional Bob Rozakis, who pointed out the Ernie Chan/Chau story in his column.

Marvel Database (http://en.marveldatabase.com/): In-depth resource for all things Marvel.

Blah Blah Blog (http://www.marvel.com/blogs/Tom%20Brevoort/): Excellent blog by longtime Marvel editor Tom Brevoort.

The Legion Omnicom (http://adventure247.blogspot.com/): Michael Grabois's in-depth examination of the Legion of Superheroes provides a number of good sources for character backgrounds like Nightcrawler and Storm.

CHAPTER TEN: WALT DISNEY COMICS

A Guide to the Carl Barks Universe (http://www.seriesam.com/barks/): Daniël van Eijmeren's expansive examination and cataloging of the work Carl Barks did for Disney's comic book line.

Ius Mentis (http://www.iusmentis.com/patents/priorart/donaldduck/): Examination of the Karl Krøyer patent case.

CHAPTER ELEVEN: VARIOUS COMIC BOOK COMPANIES

Elvis and Gladys: Elaine Dundy's acclaimed biography of Elvis Presley's early life.

The Harveyville Fun Times! (http://thft.home.att.net/): Mark Arnold's site devoted to Harvey Comics. Arnold also has a print collection of the best of the Harveyville Fun Times.

Byrne Robotics (http://www.byrnerobotics.com/): Official John Byrne Web site, with a forum that Byrne posts in and where he delivers a great deal of interesting comic knowledge.

List of Artist Names Along with Issue Numbers

(If two artists are listed, the first artist is the penciler and the second artist is the inker)

8   All Joe Shuster, *Look* Magazine (panels)

10   Joe Shuster (credited) (Likely either John Sikela or Ed Dobrotka, in reality) (comic strip)

12   Jon Bognadove and Dennis Janke, *Superman Man of Steel* #82 (cover)

20   Dan Jurgens and Brett Breeding, *Superman* #75 (cover)

27   Jack Kirby,

28   Jack Kirby

29   Alex Toth (with Curt Swan), *Limited Collectors Edition* #41 (front cover)

30   Alex Toth, *Limited Collectors Edition* #41 (back cover)

30–31   Kyle Baker, *Elseworlds 80-Page Giant* #1 (interior panels)

36   Bob Kane and Jerry Robinson, *Batman* #1 (interior panel)

38   Bob Kane and Jerry Robinson, *Batman* #1 (interior panel)

40   Sheldon Moldoff, *Batman* #160 (cover)

40   Sheldon Moldoff and Joe Giella, *Batman* #164 (cover)

43   Carmine Infantino and Joe Giella, *Detective Comics* #356 (cover)

44   Carmine Infantino and Murphy Anderson, *Batman* #181 (cover)

45   Carmine Infantino and Murphy Anderson, *Detective Comics* #359 (cover)

46   Brian Bolland, *Batman: The Killing Joke* (cover)

47   Norm Breyfogle, *Suicide Squad* #49 (cover)

47   Jerry Ordway, *Birds of Prey* #100 (cover)

52   Everett Hibbard, *All Star Comics* #3 (cover)

54   Alex Toth, *Green Lantern* #38 (cover)

57 Fred Ray, *Superman* #9 (cover)

57 C.C. Beck, *Captain Marvel Adventures* #3 (cover)

58 Gene Colan and Frank Giacoia, *Marvel Super-Heroes* #12 (cover)

59 Jeff Smith, *Shazam!: The Monster Society of Evil* (cover promo)

60 Gil Kane and Murphy Anderson, *Showcase* #34 (cover)

62 Win Mortimer, *Strange Adventures* #8 (cover)

62 Bob Brown, *Tomahawk* #102 (cover)

63 Mike Sekowsky and Murphy Anderson, *Justice League of America* #43 (cover)

64 Nick Cardy, *The Brave and the Bold* #60 (cover)

65 Ross Andru and Mike Esposito, *Wonder Woman* #129 (cover)

68 Alex Toth, *House of Secrets* #83 (interior panel)

68 Alex Toth, *House of Secrets* #83 (interior panel)

72 Rich Buckler and Frank Springer, *Black Lightning* #1 (cover)

72 Jim Aparo, *Who's Who: The Definitive Directory of the DC Universe* #3 (interior panel)

73 Alex Toth (design sheet)

74 Charles Vess, *Books of Magic* #3 (cover)

74 Thomas Taylor, *Harry Potter and the Philosopher's Stone* (cover)

75 Simon Bisley, *Doom Patrol* #42 (cover)

88 Mike Sekowsky and Murphy Anderson, *The Brave and the Bold* #28 (cover)

92 Jack Kirby and Joe Sinnott, *Fantastic Four* #49 (cover)

93 Jack Kirby and an unknown inker, *Fantastic Four* #1 (cover)

93 Jack Kirby and (most likely) George Klein, *Strange Tales* #90 (cover)

93 Jack Kirby and Sol Brodsky, *Fantastic Four* #3 (unpublished) (cover)

94 Jack Kirby and Sol Brodsky, *Fantastic Four* #3 (cover)

94 Jack Kirby and Sol Brodsky, *Fantastic Four* #3 (unpublished) (interior panels)

95 Jack Kirby and Sol Brodsky, *Fantastic Four* #3 (interior panels)

95 Jack Kirby and Sol Brodsky, *Fantastic Four* #3 (unpublished) (interior panels)

96 Jack Kirby and Sol Brodsky, *Fantastic Four* #3 (interior panels)

98 De Patie-Freling Enterprises, *Fantastic Four*

100 Stuart Immonen and Scott Koblish, *Fantastic Four* (Vol. 3) #56 (interior panels)

104 Jack Kirby, *The Adventures of the Fly* #1 (promo)

106 Steve Ditko, *Amazing Fantasy* #15 (interior panels)

110 Gil Kane, *Amazing Spider-Man* #96 (cover)

111 Neal Adams, *Green Lantern/Green Arrow* #85 (cover)

113 Al Milgrom, *Amazing Spider-Man* #290 (cover)

113 John Romita, Sr., *Amazing Spider-Man Annual* #21 (cover)

114   Mark Bagley and Sam DeLaRosa, *Venom: Lethal Protector* #1 (cover)

115   Ron Frenz and Klaus Janson, *Amazing Spider-Man* #252 (cover)

117   Ron Frenz and Bill Sienkiewicz, *What If. . . ?* #105 (cover)

127   John Buscema and Alfredo Alcala, *Hulk!* #23 (interior panels)

128   John Buscema, *The Savage She-Hulk* #1 (cover)

133   Irv Novick, *Pep Comics* #1 (cover)

134   Jack Kirby, *Captain America Comics* #1

134   Joe Simon, *Captain America Comics* #2

138   John Romita, Sr., *Captain America Comics* #77

142   Keith Pollard and Josef Rubinstein, *The Official Handbook of the Marvel Universe—Master Edition* #28 (interior panel)

145   Frank Brunner, *Man-Thing* #1 (cover)

145   Bernie Wrightson, *Swamp Thing* #1 (cover)

145–46   Ernest Schroeder, *Airboy Comics* Vol. 10 #3 (interior panel)

147   Bob Brown, *Doom Patrol* #86 (cover)

147   Jack Kirby and Paul Reinman, *X-Men* #2 (cover)

148   Neal Adams and Tom Palmer, *X-Men* #61 (cover)

149   Gil Kane and John Romita, Sr., *Amazing Spider-Man* #101 (cover)

149   Gil Kane and Dave Cockrum (both penciled different parts of the cover), *Giant-Size X-Men* #1 (cover)

150   Dave Cockrum, *Outsiders* (unpublished promotional poster)

154   John Byrne and Terry Austin, *Uncanny X-Men* #132 (interior panel)

156   John Byrne and Terry Austin, *Phoenix: The Untold Story* #1 (cover)

157   Jan Duursema and Dan Panosian, *X-Men Unlimited* #2 (interior panel)

165   Dan Taylor, *Super Hero Happy Hour* #1 (cover)

165   Dan Taylor, *Hero Happy Hour Super Special* 2004 (cover)

166   John Buscema and Joe Sinnott, *Fantastic Four* #119 (interior panels)

167   John Buscema and Joe Sinnott, *Fantastic Four* #119 (interior panels)

168   John Romita, Sr., *Hero for Hire* #1 (cover)

171   Jack Kirby and Chic Stone, *Avengers* #9 (cover)

171   Ross Andru and Mike Esposito, *Wonder Woman* #148 (cover)

171   Gil Kane and an unknown inker, *Power Man* #17 (cover)

171   Mike Grell, *All-Star Comics* #58 (cover)

172   Jack Kirby and Dan Adkins, *Avengers* #152 (cover)

173   Gil Kane and an unknown inker, *Marvel Spotlight* #32 (cover)

176   Dick Ayers, *Sgt. Fury* #8 (interior panels)

178   Barry Windsor-Smith and Johnny Verpoorten, *Conan the Barbarian* #1 (cover)